Locked Down:

poems, diary extracts and art

from the 2020 pandemic

edited by

Susan Jane Sims

poetryspace

Locked Down:

poems, diary extracts and art from the 2020 pandemic

Published in 2021

Poetry Space Ltd

Text set in Palatino Linotytpe.

Format of poem titles in line with MLA.

Section titles taken from poems included in that section.

Poetry Space Ltd Company Number 7144469

Reg. Office 2 North St, Beaminster, Dorset DT8 3DZ

Printed and bound in Great Britain by

Whitehall Printing Company, Bristol

ISBN: 978-1-909404-41-0

Locked

Down

Other Poetry Space anthologies include:

Through A Child's Eyes: Poems from World War Two, edited by Moira Andrew, 2013.

A Scream of Many Colours, edited by Moira Andrew and Susan Jane Sims, 2019.

Poetry collections by Susan Jane Sims:

Irene's Daughter, Poetry Space Ltd, 2010.

A number of things you should know, IDP, 2015.

Splitting Sunlight, Dempsey & Windle, 2019.

Also edited by Susan Jane Sims:

P.S. I have cancer: wrestling melanoma and falling in love, by Mark Sims, Poetry Space Ltd, 2018.

Poetry Space Ltd operates on a 'not for personal profit' basis and profits are used to widen participation in poetry and in some cases to benefit selected charities.

Acknowledgements

Thank you to all the contributors for giving your poems, your diary extracts, and your artwork freely to this anthology and for being so enthusiastic and encouraging about this project. Selected lines from poems form loose section headings.

The profits from sales of this anthology will go to my late son Dr Mark Sims' fund* for Cancer Research UK. Mark began fundraising when the malignant melanoma (skin cancer) he developed as a teenager spread throughout his body. He died in 2017 after a 23 month illness during which he raised awareness of cancer, particularly amongst young people, won awards for his work including a British Citizen Award and Ambassador of the Year 2016 for CRUK and inspired many people across the world. In the year after Mark's death his name appeared on The London Evening Standard's list of 1000 influential Londoners.

It feels fitting to dedicate this book to Mark as one of the consultants Mark worked with said recently that 'if Mark were here now he would be right in the thick of things doing his bit' just as his brothers, his friends and his former colleagues are right now.

*www.justgiving.com/mark-sims5

Contents

What's up with the birds?

Taking a line for a walk

Perhaps answers are yeast and rise very slowly

Something to do with love

For the vine is a form of hope rising from its root

Somehow whenever the music stops it's Wednesday

Delphinium Blue

Introduction

On New Year's Eve 2019 a new virus called COVID-19 appeared in the media. A cluster of cases had occurred in Wuhan, China. By January 2020, China had reported the first death. From the UK we watched in alarm and wonder as cases started to occur outside China and very soon across the world. On the 23rd March 2020 UK Prime Minister, Boris Johnson made a historic speech telling all citizens that they must stay at home and work from home where possible, unless in key roles. Within a few days all non-essential businesses including the cafe in Dorset I run with my husband Chris were ordered to close. Other European countries had already locked down.

This anthology offers a glimpse into the disrupted lives of those forced to stay at home, wherever they are in the world and a glimpse into the challenging working environment of those known as frontline workers. It also explores the grief, the pain, the loneliness and the frustration caused by this pandemic through the eyes of observers and those touched directly by the virus.

The material is presented in loose chronological order from Spring through to the beginning of Autumn 2020. The final poems look forward to society getting back to some sort of normality though at the point of publication none of us have a clear idea of when that will be.

Susan Jane Sims, January 2021

What's up with the birds?

Crow

Crow, low across the meadow grass
waits on the wall
and returns.

Black, wings outstretched,
profoundly present;
yet evoking
a strange absence.

Absorbed,
I am not there.

Peter Reason

Crow - Sarah Gillespie

Crows Gather

Crows caw and build nests,
balls of twigs in a bare tree.
Sound is rough and ugly
but they're unaware of
closed doors, shop queues,
loo rolls and the round red sphere.

They fly here and there sounding
off, carry sticks much longer
than themselves. One carries
a suet ball, prize from the garden.
The colony grows, company
accepted, crowds allowed,

no measuring of distance,
no waiting and taking turns.
Soon eggs will be laid and
incubated. More black flights
tomorrow, more jubilant
gatherings in the treetops.

Judy Dinnen

Seventh Day
Louis MacNeice, Sunday Morning

Groggy from the night before,
you make your way to Tesco to pick up
Ragout, Lamb Biriani, Prosecco.
If you have time, you take the car
to be cleansed before you drive
Carol and the kids through sardined roads
to *The Packsaddle* for lunch. It's another
Sunday, but it's a day off at least.

Only the very elderly seem to hear the bells
which summon, whom to what?

Robin Thomas

COVID-19, 25 February 2020

We are naive, coronavirus virgins,
as it were, for this one, anyway –
something's happened, weaponised the germ
between the pangolin, the bat, the civet cat

and so we watch, and wait, and listen, while
the science circus trundles into town
– lives to be saved, careers to be made
– and hitherto unknown becomes the norm.

Looks like a harvest moon, a sea anemone.
Who gets it, how, where from, what does it do?
What makes it better, anything at all?
China sneezes; will we all fall down?

Skies quiet, trade abandoned, shops out of stock;
we burrow down, to hibernate until it goes away
while leaders hope that history will recall
their prudence, how they stared the virus out.

Its name avoids the stigma of a national link
just notes the year when it appeared, when someone
noticed something going on, and spoke
but had his collar felt; he'd rocked the boat.

Stuart Handysides

The Train: 1993, 2020

The Russian train has two young women guides,
Katya, slim Helen. Flowered shirt-cloth hides
paunches on the young Mafia. Knives slide
all day on the potato-peeler's knee
between compartments. Sasha grins, strides past,
six feet of engineer. Steam-whistles blast.
The quiet, helpful man who boarded last,
with fluent German, may be KGB.

We see the wooden towns. We glimpse a moose,
churches with incense, dead pools like a bruise
by slender broken birches. Who would choose
to live here? Fresh food for her child to eat
is Helen's aim. Why, on the final day
do sobs shake her small breasts, to the train's sway?
Sasha, shrunk suddenly, stows tools away
before he meets the murderous Moscow street.

***

Sickness. Each night I board, in home-locked dream,
a fearful train. A boy in bundled green
who has no papers, leaps out, rolls down scree,
races past startled cows. The wet glass streams,
I grip my silvered strip of pills. I know
I must find the young girl, whose vivid glow
means fever. Calm, awake, would I do so?
I doubt it. We are better in our dreams.

I wake, then shiver. The March light blows wild.
How many died? How old is Helen's child?
I must feed cats, next, count the tinned peas, piled

against our hungers, the forgotten rain.
I could use Sasha's tools. Who will bring pills?
In each room sleepers wake, while pure sun spills.
The radio leaks facts. The kettle fills.
Rocked deeper, scared, we still must ride this train.

Alison Brackenbury

A Pandemonium of Parrots

This window is a portal and conversations stutter
between the parakeets and the radio
the callers on the line pouring their sadness
into the ears of Jeremy Vine and a million
listeners stirring a cup of tea.

The news comes thick and fast
and it hurts to listen to the stories coming
from deep in the throat, farewells denied, bedside
goodbyes uttered over the phone.
'We told him that we loved him', the caller's
voice cracked on the line, 'the girls too,
they're just old enough to understand
he won't be coming home.'

The birds are even louder now the streets
no longer scream. It's spring and the air
is filled with jays, wood-pigeons, herring-gulls,
crows. Parakeets shoot like arrows from the trees.
'I'm sorry for your loss, I'm sorry for your loss.'
Stories come more frequently, another broken soul
this one was just a boy, just a boy.

My telephone brings my mother's voice, she's
84, alone. Her scattered reminiscences of other times,
another country, itself in lockdown now; unimaginable
all that sun, where parakeets and parrots bright as zinnias
anoint the sky ... her scattered reminiscences sparkle
my isolated air, we are in a bubble she and I.
I tell her about the parakeets. 'Chin up,' she says,
'Chin up. This too will pass. This too will pass.'

Maggie Harris

Morning

The guardian angel put on his shoes
                  did not even drink water
                  but fed the cat

                  said goodbye to his mother

He adjusted his suit
He got into the underground

    greeted visiting beggars
    and losers

He opened the digits of the books
    in a London office building

He will call later:
Systems of human affairs close at twelve o'clock

Anna Maria Mickiewicz

Masqued

The meat, two veg, come in a box,
a corrugated lover's knot,
new menu with the change of clocks,
less calories, more friends beside.
More folk are shouting, by-pass route -
the village lads, silent till now -
though street messages over hedge,
the walls are smashed, now voice, not mail.

Though masks are taught, ear, nose and throat,
the dreaded sphere - no entry here -
as if at ball, the masque is dropped,
the dance card fills, strange signatures.
The vacant space, a bubble wrap
ensures she recalls pace before,
when, frame retained, with measured steps
she waltzed, while pleats swished, skirting air.

Her carer now brings daily aid,
unwitting entry, hidden plague,
all visits paid along the road,
as if the lintels blood mark daubed.
Welled grief at lonely untouched pass,
pants heaving breast, her gasps for air,
assert his love beyond the call,
the dance resumed, shared meeting phase.

Stephen Kingsnorth

Memories of the Garden of Eden

The Blackbird in the bare Wisteria
against the wall sings a piece of Eden:
his song, sounding so impromptu, spills out
exuberantly, while the singer himself
takes it easy. We hear it where we are,
not in the bird's demesne – exiled from it.

In early March at the time of *Covid*
a reference-point like the Blackbird's song
reminds us of separating from Eden,
finding, on leaving, that it wasn't perfect –
that, solid as a statue or stone fountain
at the centre of the garden, there was pain.

In his notes, we hear grief. As people do.
Pain has been ascribed to certain music:
Nightingales – so tremulous, heart-broken …
The Blackbird has his territory, his song.
Now it seems other-worldly. Tomorrow,
we'll know the singer better: his music ours.

Dilys Wood

Tree - Alanna McIntyre

Developed through multimedia and layering

What's Up with the Birds?

What's up with the birds
round my way?
Hardly venturing out.

What's up with the birds?

They disappeared for weeks
round my way.
Hardly a one to be found.

What's up with the birds?

The council cut back all the trees
round my way.
Maybe the birds were afraid?

Is that what's up with the birds?

A pigeon, a crow, is all I've seen
and a little chittering can be heard
but even the dug-over garden's empty,
no watchers for juicy bugs and worms.

What's come over the birds
round my way?
Fled to Eden now humanity's closed?

Is that what's become of the birds?

Anne Stewart

Pandemic

I'm doing my best not to tap into websites,
the latest deaths, the rising numbers,
doing my best to just listen

to the shuddering world and the dark
March trees, to how it feels to be here

in the moment history will write about
in a way we can't know - a time of change
perhaps, of priorities altering

like the winds from Wuhan and London, Madrid and Milan
pushing us towards a new humility,
lesson we need to learn so many times

Dorothy Baird

Kindergarten 1

19th March 2020

Here is a festival of flowers;
children in a garden playing in winter drizzle,
or seated on logs, drinking milk,
holding on to each other, laughing.
The whole world is full of fear.

A-tishoo, a-tishoo, we all fall down.
I write a prayer in my notebook.
Please God, keep them safe.

Denise Bennett

Haiku in Lockdown

March 2020

1
Sun under bare trees –
in the wind a crowd
of primroses, shivering.

2
Across the street a red van
pulls up. Who's getting what
from whom? I must know!

3
Distant lawn mower
drones over shaggy grass -
from stillness, a voice!

4
Dark skeleton of
tree, you lie flat in the grass
– the magic of shadow.

5
We played in the park -
remember the green see-saw -
how it tipped, like hope.

6
Lost underground since
last spring, early purple orchid,
hello again!

7
A red handbag slumps
in a corner abandoned.
It longs to go out.

Pam Zinnemann-Hope

Relentlessly We Are Hammered with Our Impending Death

When they bundled the migrants into a van
they wore masks, didn't care cameras were recording.

Like Greek Gods we are suspended
above a roadside between borders.

We no longer mourn for another drowned boy
we are impervious to water.

On Lesbos there is fighting, fear
the ferry departs without offering safe haven.

On the Cruise Liner Princess staff to tourist 1:2
Infection 17:2. People stay in their rooms.

Helicopters visit the ship - Contain! Contain! Contain!
Drop off hope.

Morag Kiziewicz

Ithaca

The evening before lockdown
  we take a drive to Severn Beach to walk the dog
  the final time we'll leave the city
  the final time we'll see 'the sea'
  for who knows how long
  and we park by the boarded-up café
  gaze out over mud flats and motorway traffic
  migratory birds en route
  for northern breeding grounds

Why don't we pretend this is Greece, you say
  as the sun sets on Ithaca over the river
  and early next morning when I wake up
  I make out a headland of cloud through the dawn
  a rising tide

Deborah Harvey

Taking Stock

The force that through the green fuse drives the flower
Drives my green age; that blasts the roots of trees
is my destroyer.

Dylan Thomas

We could say this new virus
is our retribution, that nature now is
fighting back, but nature always does fight back
with teeth and claws, and with rebirth.

Everything that lives is hellbent on living. The force
that drives the panic buy is the force that drives green shoots
through an earth scorched by fire or frozen by ice.
The same force kept my son Mark fighting his way through
cancer. The same force enabled cancer to destroy.

Slow down. Take stock. That's my advice if it's of any worth.
Think of those for whom hunger is an everyday experience;
those for whom pain is common place, isolation the norm.

Let's make our mouthfuls of food last, not rush out for more.
Let's make every word we have the privilege of uttering,
kind ones.

Susan Jane Sims

A Kindness: Wendy Halsted

St Mary's Street Bakery, March 2020

We obey the pavement's pink chalk stripes,
two metres apart. We play with our phones
to pass the time - or pitch a few words underarm,

like soft tennis balls, to the next in line.
It's easy to talk to strangers, these strange days.
Something has loosened our tongues,

not just a shared desire for seeded sourdough
and cardamom twists, bagels and bostock,
sanctioned sunlight and clean, yeasty air.

I sigh at the scent from the open bakery door.
Behind me, a man asks, *What can you smell?*
I tell him, *Croissants, brioche, hot cross buns,*

but that's not all. What I smell is sweet
as a baby's head after sleep, soft as its feet.

It is fresh as the blackbird's steady serenade
this Saturday morning on St Mary's Street.

I smell the small warm realities we can tuck
under one arm and take, contented, home.

Sarah Mnatzaganian

Waiting for the Next Word

It was,
we thought, just the B-word,
a silence hanging over the table,
dividing friend from friend, turning
the body politic into a body folly-sick.
The border issue, between leave & remain
the non-events, on the 31st, the 30th, 31st again.

Before
we'd caught our breath, C,
had grabbed the last toilet rolls,
had emptied the pubs, cafes, theatres,
threatened with every cough and suspect
door-handle. An endless rattle of no other news,
lock-down, the hockey-stick lift in hospital cases.

Now,
we fear, there's the D-word.
He tries not to rattle as he strides
under his black robes, or let the glint
off his long, notched blade catch our eyes.
Still he watches from empty sockets and grins
whirling his new crown of a trillion bristling gems.

And
if we EVER get to the E-word,
will that be Ecstasy, hooray, still here!?
Empathy, with those who've been bereaved?
or simply Emptiness, vacant chairs in committee,
homes unoccupied, save for desolate cats and dogs,
while nurses fold clean linen on left-over hospital beds?

Michael Hutchinson

Writing and Painting in Covid-19

With my paint brush I will paint violence,
an oil painting of unrecognisable objects
timebomb - Covid-19
in hospitals, nursing homes
social gatherings, framed and endorsed
by Francis Bacon, Kandinsky and Picasso.
My pencil will write a modern classic
a subculture of violence -
Covid-19 Clockwork Orange
unreal social distancing, no hanging out
at the bars, shops, a borstal to reform Covid-19.
Covid-19 is rooted in fairy-tale notoriety
a children's book, come over to my house:
built of wood, straw and bricks.

Johanna Boal

The Stella Fella Code of Conduct

The Chief of Lads looked out at the crowd
and addressed his townsfolk.

Tomorrow we'll gather all the wheelchairs
in the square. We'll lift them onto the stage,
get a good look at them.

I'll pass out the beers,
six each in a white carrier bag.

On my command, point at them.
Shout, *oi, look at me.*
If they don't comply walk up to them
put your face into theirs, shower them
in Stella phlegm.

Be as aggressive as possible.
I'm not staying in for you.
I don't give a fuck
if you get it.

Don't forget the uniform.
Tops off lads, shorts on.
Adidas on display.

Strain the sinews, get that skin tight,
show them how big you are.

Stephen Lightbown

Last Straw

'seems like I'm not alone in being alone' (Sting: Message in a Bottle)

A morning call, some thirty years ago
the police, requiring me to come
and put my stamp on what they knew.

The warden would have let them know;
no answer at the door, they'd broken in
the coroner would need to hear.

I'd seen him only recently
at surgery, then at home,
a barren first floor flat

his chesty cough not yet improved
the pub across the road, his lifeline,
out of reach for now.

An empty whisky bottle by the bed
a Tesco plastic bag, knotted roughly
where his head should be.

Impetuous, impatient man, I thought,
wore my grim face, did what I had to do
returned to colleagues, wife and kids.

Stuart Handysides

Sleeping Spell

Two thirty, three seventeen.
I never used to see these numbers,
rose from a black hole of sleep
ready to chase down the day.

Now, though my eyes are shut
as tight as blackout blinds,
the numbers still shine through.
Translated into words
they batter me with questions.

Will she get that promised job?
Will their love survive this separation?
How will our world be changed?

They tell the sleepless soldiers not to think
just to repeat *don't think.*

But, in the Victorian theatre of my mind,
up in the gods I can recite the spell
while on the gas-lit stage
I let go of a child's hand,
cannot tell an old man that I love him.

Four ten, five fifty three.

Ann Preston

6AM

and the white skim of sleep
over the park, its silence untouched
by newly awakened grass,

by trees speckling the sky
with the green of folded leaves,
stops me at the landing window.

If I could dip my mind into the green
outside maybe the anxieties
clinging like strands of cleaver,

would wash away. Near the stream:
a runner - I envy his supple legs.
He barely touches the stillness,

neither does the fox that's appeared
in our garden from nowhere.
His reddish coat is as fierce as fire,

his eyes are ungiving as granite
and as he snuffles at the ground, sniffs
a path across the lawn

his disregard for property unnerves me.
He's slipped into next door's jungle
when a bank of cloud elongates

and parts like a pair of immense lips.
At once a liquid gold pours out.
It streams through branch

and fence into our garden,
my body. Day is about to bloom
but I want to halt it,

to keep the lone runner
in the silence of the park,
keep the fox, his wild glory.

Myra Schneider

High Tide in the Morning

The moon controls more than our tides
    pulls at more than Earth's deep troughs
sloshing brims
        crumbling cliffs to dissolve like tablets
salted turbulence
ceaseless fussing of a worrier's hands

just like these children
          who surge into my room, my bed
       crash into my heart, flood me with chatter
    their energies zingy as sea spray.

We cannot leave this house
       awash with unfinished projects
          dirty socks
    scrunched up sheets of abandoned drawings.

I'm scrolling news that's rolling in
            story upon story
so many names, so many
        lung-stinging   suffocating   splashes

and still feeds are filtered to the brightest of colours
    still we lose hours
      gazing at reflections   mirrored in lakes

when we've   all of us   blown far out to sea

    swung on each wave at the whim of the moon.

Under sunlit   blustering
        windswept skies

we cast off

into this day
      its dip and swell
                        into its lull

   helming as best we can.

Zannah Kearns

Slowing Down

I am growing to love,
spaced out queues,
pavement dreaming;
the sky above a mosaic
in a hundred shades of white and blue.

I am growing to love
my garden, everyday a
subtle change, blossom sweet
and full, blanketing the grass
in a tight weave.

I am growing to love, lazy mornings,
scalding jam, watching froth rise.

Susan Jane Sims

Lockdown Writings
27/3/20

I made a bubble,
and now they tell me I must live in it.

I'm glad it's a good bubble –
it took years to make

and I often got it wrong.
But the final result was worth the effort.

I love my bubble.

I might stay in it forever.

Jo Waterworth

In these days

I'm turning to jazz.
Trying not to play the obvious.
Looking for a harmony in the altered
Rhythms and times that are new to me.

I'm looking for a hook to hang my hat.
I'm looking for the sweet note
That resolves the ragged-time discordant moan,
The jangling tone, of the ten o'clock news.

Music is my alchemy,
That secret note or harmony
Might replace through improvisation
The diminished by augmentation.

These are my jazz days.
Born out of prohibition.
'Summertime and the living's' –
Suspended, flattened, hanging in the balance.
These are my Jazz days.

Words by David Greenwood, illustration by Susan Greenwood

48

Swans in Lockdown

A notice on the DIY says 'Panic buyers welcome'.
By the supermarket car-park a swan mounts guard
beside a drainage outlet. On the bank there's a
smudge like dirty snow. Inside the shop,
a drift of swans on plastic wrappers threatens to wipe out
shoppers in an avalanche of toilet rolls.

Stocked up on toilet rolls and given up on hand-wash
I creep alongside a tyre repair man's van -
'No-one holds a patch on us' - to look for the swan's nest.
It is just beyond the railings, wedged against
a dead willow tree swept by Macdonald's wrappers,
spattered by red cartridges of vodka and cola cans.

The mother bird preens in watery sunlight,
her neck grubby as if she needs to take a dip.
She shifts cramped wings, stretches a black leg,
tilts to one side and there they are -
five perfect eggs.

The swans are in lockdown too.
Last year, out of eight cygnets,
only one survived.

Ann Preston

Clinical Material

We loved being sent away
to district generals in the sticks –
real pathology there, they said
clinical signs, stuff you read about

not the Sunday-best patients
here for benediction, laying-on of hands
by the prof who saved them, long ago,
and gave his name to something never seen before

– the hospitals in towns you'd never think
of visiting, hadn't known were there
where an aged alumnus
kindly kept a link alive

and where they made you welcome
and let you practise as you learned
junior but accepted casuals
fed and comforted in the mess

a novelty to patients newly ill
who sometimes called you doctor
and you hastily demurred
remembering your place.

The murmurs, rubs and masses
that you found – no longer just in books –
once auscultated, seen, palpated
stayed with you for life.

And now, too long retired to get hauled back
it is for others – seasoned docs
and those still fresh from school –
to make their names on something new.

There are no well-thumbed monographs.
They quickly share online what they have seen
learn what the virus does, to whom, and what to do
– learn to care through muffled speech and eyes alone.

Stuart Handysides

Millennium Square, Bristol - Chris Sims

The Littlest among Us

are being taught to wash their hands
to the Happy Birthday song
sung twice over.

The rest of us adopt our own tunes
of twenty second duration.
The supermarket shelves are empty;

the pubs and city squares silent
after the last ditch deluge
of f...the virus drinking.

We sit at home and wait
for a fever, or a cough
the start of something scary.

We talk of secretly breaking out
to meet with others
like naughty school children.

Susan Jane Sims

Where Is St George When We Need Him?

The dragon crept up on us
leaving its slimy trail over
countries in its wake.

It snarled just enough to arouse
a slight frisson of fear, then curled
its long sharp tail around its body

and considered where, in the absence
of the frail virgins it had hoped for,
it would attack first.

Vicious teeth and claws snapped
at me, almost claimed me. I heard
its angry growl as I slipped away

leaving all my health and strength,
as a maiden's modest garments,
in a pile outside his lair.

Letting out a blast of angry fire, he
continued to rampage throughout
our land, intent on slaughter

caught my unsuspecting brother
and several of my friends
and would not let them go.

So where is St George now?
Maybe we no longer need
his story, because this time

it will be the ordinary goodness
of friends and neighbours that will
save us, slay the dragon.

Alwyn Marriage

Time Lapse

In the time it takes my mother
    to press down with her good foot
    inch herself up the mattress

a blurred helicopter red through rain
    has clattered over the hospital roof
    and come in to land

and someone in an oxygen mask
    is trolleyed up the path
    into Accident and Emergency.

Back in her room
    it could be morning or evening
    perhaps it has taken one hour or twelve

for the nurse to swing round my mother's legs
    and ease her swollen feet
    into her fur-trimmed slippers

or for a damp and wrinkled head
    to push its way through tearing flesh
    and another hear the cry that's new and ages old.

My mother sways on her pinned hip grips her zimmer
    as the hospital bends to its endless task
    of manufacturing ghosts.

Deborah Harvey

In Lockdown

your back gate is half open   in lockdown
the sun has stunned next door's grass   in lockdown
hedges and trees are opening their billion green hands

in lockdown   the lift is afraid
in lockdown   the stairways are panicky
both kids at once want your phone to call their friend

in lockdown   birds cross our windows   in lockdown
the sky outside is drinkable blue   in lockdown
the night is peopled its moons familiar and you wake

in lockdown   each night map turns and forgets us
in lockdown   I think I see you come round the corner
to whistles and pans and doors unlocking their hands

Dominic Fisher

Before They Wake

Red sun hangs perfect, terrible as war,
the blink of grief, the glass which holds no more.
Then gold throbs, the unbearable sun's eye,
magnolia whitens, boiler smoke streams by
till lowered clouds and muffled radiance give
that dull but blessed light by which we live.

Alison Brackenbury

Taking a line for a walk

4:50 in the Afternoon

and I'm heading east.
Two skeins of geese, the moon,
a tissue paper sky, the sun
behind me. The strangeness
of these last months belongs
to a far-fetched world. This loveliness
is mine to enjoy for a while.
This traffic jam allows me.

A glut of seagulls flocks by. The sun
has moved. The moon, stalwart
beauty, stays with me – a kindness,
a fair companion for a while,
as I – as we all must now –
negotiate the tilted world.

Anne Stewart

Below the Water Lily

I find my rhythm, the slow beat
of minims. I hear the music
of a hundred years, half hidden
promises of unexpected cadences.

I find my soul, waiting patiently
to say its name. I ask it questions.
Hold its murmured answers.
I live the silence, find there
new sighs and vibrations.

I open a poem, let it walk through my veins.
I read a psalm, touch the fringes
of its ancient wisdom. I look beneath
the beauty of the water lily.

I dive below the upbeat of my heart,
measure the meaning of new syllables.
I write in the mystery depths
of lost spaces, sense a new presence.

I listen between the words
of a neighbour's tale. From
afar, I hold her anxious hand,
promise bread and wine - next year.

Judy Dinnen

Without a Light

There are walls too high to climb.
No doors. No gates. No breaches anywhere.

There are forests that seem impenetrable
and yet, you put your faith in these.

It's possible to walk a forest's edge for days, years
and find your every way is blocked.
Each morning's path a circle back to night.

Then, just once, the moonlight delivers
full and bright, in line with every cliché,
a chink, let's say, between two giant pines.

You enter and wait until your eyes adjust.
Here, even the shadows disappear.
You are standing on a path of sorts.
Not the fabled one with light at the end.
This is ill defined.
Enough to set one foot
in front of the other.
Nothing more.

You take it.

Eileen Anne Gordon

Lockdown Writings

30/3/20

We are waiting.
Bright morning sunshine
and brisk cold winds
and everywhere birdsong
and the bursting of buds
and the hopeful planting of seeds
and the unaccustomed hush
all scream at us LIFE!
Life,
life.
We are waiting for the surge of deaths.

Jo Waterworth

Lockdown, Lockdown, It's the Only Game in Town

Lockdown, lockdown, it's the only game in town
Where you are your own jailer, trusty and screw,
The decisions you make, they are up to you.
It is house arrest, but without the tagging
After so many weeks your morale maybe flagging
Lockdown, lockdown, it's the only game in town.
You are the parole board. You could grant a reprieve.
But where would you go? You know you can't leave.
Your walks cut a groove, as you circle the garden
If you don't do it daily, your arteries will harden.
Lockdown, lockdown, it's the only game in town
You must remember to dress for the video call
To exchange your news, which is bugger all.
For now, we must dream of those treks in the hills
Of dining out and other such thrills.

We know this will end,
What we don't know is when.

David C. Johnson

23/04/2020 – The First Diary Entry of an English Teacher in Lockdown

The blank page. That old friend. Or enemy? Rival? Is that a thing in writing? God knows I've waited so long to sit and write this and now here I am. Words pouring onto the page. It feels good. Fluid. Like water. As essential as water? Are all writers poets? I don't know. Is that poetic? Or does it just want to be poetic? How long am I going to write for? I promised myself 30 mins a day and I think I could probably fill it. This is a kind of therapy isn't it. No audience. Hey, check that out, a question with no question mark. Sometimes I teach the kids to write Pages or Free Writing. They love it mostly. Being allowed to write for the sake of it. For the sake of talking. The weight of a cheap biro in their hands. The sound of ballpoint pens furiously tearing into the page. I do miss that. The teaching I mean. Actually seeing my kids.

I can hear Andy laughing upstairs. It's gone 10pm and he's still in a meeting with his career coach. God love that man, he's a tryer. Not many people who would cut themselves in half to be body beautiful. But that is Andy, not someone to go by halves. Yet, so quick to open himself up and dig out the "ugly". Moving on moving on. Pushing forward. Always pushing. To be the best, the funniest, most attractive, most outrageous. He does make me laugh. There's a metaphor in there somewhere. Cuts himself open to be body beautiful. Carves the inside out. And that's what he did really. Released from the cocoon of bandages like a butterfly. All the colours of the rainbow. I am proud of him.

Been writing for 10 minutes and it feels like infinity and it feels like nothing. Is it cheating if I check the time, all the time? My writing is always filled with questions when I'm writing as me. My anxiety seeping through. Like blood onto the page. Staining in small round symbols. This is a life-blood for me. A lifeline. Always back to base. Black. To writing. Somehow, here. No matter how far I stray. Was I born a writer? Or a talker? A story-teller? A silver-smithed tongue-wagger? Extensively metaphorical lolly-gagger? Maybe it is poetry after all. Maybe I just can't help myself. Maybe it's Maybelline? Maybe I should go back to the high street. Am I so entrenched in this commodified world and way of existing that these crass tag-lines invade even my most intimate thoughts?

Another question. Good grief. Another 5 minutes passed. 5 minutes of my life. Am I taking in or letting go? Is my cup full to pour from? Does it need to be when I'm writing? I can catch these thoughts, put them onto paper and keep them. No need to store them in my head where they float around aimlessly, relentlessly, clinging on, desperate not to be forgotten. Like the others. The ideas. That one I had about Greek gods or stories? I didn't write it down and now it's a half-formed memory. An idea I had that won't become an idea again and will fade over time into the distant fog of my mind to be replaced by another. And will the other one be better? I guess we'll never know. Different, maybe. Informed by it. Fed by it. By the pain and the rejection and the holding on. Red raw fingers pushing and pushing. Ensuring my future. Writing again. Blood on my hands. Lady Macbeth. Out damned spot, out I say! Will all of Neptune's waters ever wash these hands clean? Clean clean clean. Clean of the child. The nightmares. The woman. The reality. The electricity. The woman. The reality. The words. Are they clean? Are they clean? Are they clean?

Is this a poem? Or a melody? A tragedy. 4 minutes gone. Rocking with the rhythm. Maybe it's flow, maybe it's madness. A few minutes in my mind. Calm. Not quite. Can't capture the words quickly enough. They just flow and fall and my hands stumble.

Teddy is barking. Some damn bird in the garden making a noise no doubt. He is so intuitive. He knows when I need him. Sat by my feet earlier. I wanted to say for 20 minutes but the truth is I don't check the time with him. An indeterminate, indefinite amount of time. His skin on mine. Heart beat against my chest. Breath on my ear. White. Pure.

3 minutes more and then I'm done. I might need to start with 20 minutes because this is infinitely hard and easy but hard. And reading over my own words. The madness. The love and the pain and the words. I don't know, I think it will be hard. Digging for the gems. Do I need to do that? Maybe not. Maybe this is just for me. The unlock. The key. A space to write and to be. Funny, this rhyme, always seems to bubble under my words. Not necessarily something I'm aiming for and yet it comes to be? Maybe it *is* poetry. Or something grey. Uncomfortable and in-between? How can I enjoy these things when I am so clear cut? A Virgo rising. Or is it Libra? One or the other. A perfectionist, methodical, organised and clean. Not the messy, wishy-washy Pisces that sits on my sun sign and blocks out the clarity. Emotions, yes. But not strategy.

0 mins left. Fin. See you tomorrow Pages. Or Diary. Xxx

Rosie Georgiou

The Seven Deadly Sins - Mark Pender

Covid-19

Remember 'close', remember rubbing shoulders with strangers?–
was it good to jostle in a crowd, to range side by side
on gaudy beach-mats, the whiff of someone's sun-cream or ice-cream
drifting by, and someone else stepping over our stretched legs?

Have we come to love 'separateness', or do we wish for
crammed-tight tube-trains, lifts at full capacity – that brief
warm intimacy, then soaring still with one other person,
as if married to this one for a minute, then divorced.

Nodding to strangers at two metres distance, I ask how much
these once-seen persons have meant to me? The start of something
that came to nothing? A glance confirming a prejudice?
I mutter about, 'The possibilities of strangers' …

At nights, people with no past history enter my dreams –
passers-by, unnoticed on the street, faces registered
without a conscious thought, these are close companions
of the dream-story … Somehow, our brain-cells cannibalise

every moment in a crowd, all the check-ins, check-outs,
all the gatherings of faces. 'I see you', I signal
to the 'forbidden fruit' at twice-arm's-length. I know – we know –
about 'on-hold', and hoping to be 'close' with strangers again.

Dilys Wood

Prescience

After a while
        I no longer listen to my favourite songs

because suddenly each one's been written
        for this contingency

while the poems I've loved
        peel off their masks

turn to face me in their bruised
        and swollen skin

Deborah Harvey

Calendar Kept in a Time of Crisis

MARCH

Friday 13th   There's a near Full Moon out there but not always
visible. The day when it is clear there will be major
change.

Sat 14th.   Staying in to sort. My heart-shaped earring tree
from Gill has pairs hanging neatly.

Sun 15th   The rocket in Top Polytunnel is plentiful and I pick
a big bunch.

Mon 16th   Bright blue skies and a walk on the river towpath.

Tues 17th   The bench on the Skyline with the Eleanor Duse
(1859-1924) quote:
*'If a blade of grass springing up in the fields
has the power to move you, rejoice for your
soul is alive.'*

Wed 18th   A blue haze of flowers on the slopes below Rainbow
Wood House.

Thurs 19th   At Dry Arch picking kale with frilly leaves,
spangled with raindrops.

Fri 20th.   Two cheerful gardeners work to clear a slope of
shrubbery, feeding the fire below, just in view of
Shaft Road.

Sat 21st   The wind-blown daffodils that I put I put in a vase
scent the dark warm living room.

Sun 22nd   All the yellow on shrubs and flowers sing out for

Mother's Day. The top-most branches of bare trees catch the sunset with a tangerine glow.

Mon 23rd   Sun-warmed mossy seat on the log where I pause for a picnic.

Tues 24th   In Rainbow Woods there are hosts of daffodils.

Wed. 25th   Evening light and morning light equally enchanting.

Thu 26th   A beekeeper lifts the lid of a single hive in a garden singing with daffodils – a yellow blaze.

Fri 27th   Stars in a clear sky but four of them seem to be moving – a convoy of helicopters or a bevy of satellites or a shower of meteors?

Sat 28th   Children put rainbow pictures in windows and there are hearts and stars with rainbows on the railings at school.

Sun 29th   [A shifting of tectonic plates – News at One]
Cold wind across the fields where sheep graze.
Then they all start off in one direction.

Mon 30th   A pair of birds-of-prey loop and circle below The Balcony Walk on the Skyline in Bath – sparrowhawks who disappear after a while...

Tue 31st   A broad light silvers the doves which rise and fall above Monkton Combe village, sometimes they seem like triangles, turning and looping in unison.

Verona Bass

COVID-19

Dance Macabre
Pink in early Spring
this mausoleum –
parched, yet brimming over.

BC/AD
A plague of locusts.
Bodies packed tight,
out of sight.

Maureen Weldon

Just a Walk in the Park

After five great years together,
We are separated now.
Torn apart by invisible force,
You in your castle, me in mine.

The well-made rope that binds us
Is taut and contact strained
And yet like secret lovers
We meet every day.

A walk in the park, though still apart
We feed wild birds
And sometimes, if we're lucky,
They perch on treat-wielding hands.

Today we heard then spotted
A woodpecker in the trees.
Something to share in our phone calls
Until this present danger has passed.

Adele V. Robinson

Taking a Line for a Walk - Beverley Ferguson

Lockdown Writings
3/4/20

Another Quiet day

Mr Blackbird announces the dawn
as he will when we are gone.
The interrupted night is over,
 the endless day begins —
a cavernous sack to fill with activity,
punctuating the hours with tea.
Mr Blackbird announces his claim
to this time and place:
let him have it.

Jo Waterworth

Technological Limits

I'm grateful to WhatsApp, Skype and Zoom
for keeping us connected, love the fact
that I can see your face, the living fire
that lights your eyes up as you share
news every day, from your living room.

Maybe we even talk for longer
at this distance than we would
dashing in and out of busy lives.
For that I'm grateful, and appreciate
it's helping me recover and get stronger.

But, oh, I miss the touch of human hand,
yearn for a hug, knowing I'll have to wait
to be released from lock-down before I feel
the warmth of human flesh on flesh. Although
we're far apart, I know you understand.

Alwyn Marriage

Because Carole

Carole says the hardest thing is touch, not being able…
to touch her daughter, her grandkids, and it's a
fundamental urge. I say, because I haven't been touched
for so long, I haven't …missed it. And because we're
life-long friends, we wonder about this…difference of
ours. Then I wonder, if I'd had that someone else made
from my own body cells and I'd held that someone to
me their whole life, if I'd suckled, bathed and cuddled
them as they grew - because of all that, would I feel
differently now?

Because when we meet, Carole & I sit entwined and
watch telly and it's nice, that physical sensation…of
being loved and knowing someone so well, you feel at
ease in their arms.

I don't miss it. Not like I did when I was younger and
had sex, but that was different and not for a long time
now. Because of that, it made me think about what I do
miss…have missed these last strange months. Because
I'm a cat person, I admit stroking one would have eased
my isolation and at the same time I would've been able
to talk to my cat and it would have given me attention,
someone to come home to and care for.

I realise for me, it's someone to touch words with,
explore ideas with and even over the phone, talking to
her was like being hugged, because we could say these
things and wonder about stuff together. Just for half
hour or so - our minds cuddled.

Rachael Clyne

Social Distancing

They haven't hugged for a month
and the conversation stalls now
because she has no news to colour his days
and she has to shout because there's
two metres between them and
his hearing aids need adjusting.

Are even cinemas closed? he asks
for the umpteenth time and shakes
his head when she tells him again
they are. *Not even
in the war..* he says.

On the way out, she opens the door
with her sleeve-covered hand and smiles
across the distance he wants to close
and she has to maintain, pushing back
against thousands of years of evolution
and the magnetism of family.

He's over ninety, there isn't room
in his brain for this, not when he's come through
scarlet fever and diphtheria and the threat of TB
not when he remembers no antibiotics
and money behind the clock for the doctor
and the rifle he carried in a tram
to army cadet practice at the age of 17
loaded with bullets. Nothing
closed the cinemas or the doctors then. Nothing
stopped a neighbour popping over
for a cup of tea. Nothing stopped

an old man hugging his daughter.

Dorothy Baird

At Bushy Park - Daniel Benson

Missing

Once I saw two red deer, flanks so close, running to the sea
straight as a die, no tracks back, hooved sand to
surf. *Touch.* Once I read that a poppy calyx learns insect
wings, each coveted beat memorised for more. *Touch.* Once
I heard that winter moonlight pools zooplankton, oh the lack
of mystical intimacy. *Touch.* I sit here by an open window,
a collage of lockdown sounds seeping in from streets,
wondering how hot asphalt would feel beneath my feet
now. *Touch.* Like my childhood run from promenade to
beach, hopping squirm-toed quick, tar prints on our towels,
traces. *Touch.* How water lipped my longing teenage thighs
in some preordained way. *Touch.* How my age-blind
gramps tapped flat-fingered from room to room, and his
smooth knowing kettle , waiting. *Touch.* When all this is
over, when my door opens and the infinite possibilities of
summer light flood in, I'll learn once more dear heart. *Touch.*
I will try to go slowly so as not to lose anyone. Try to be still.

Mary Gilonne

Ego and Id

Isolated, locked down and confined
whilst the governments roll out 5G
Impoverished and certificated
with machine guns in the market place

A rare "bonjour" - looks could kill
Street-crossing avoidance
Bonhomie has bombed
Our come-uppance is coming up

Soaring with the sparrowhawk in pristine skies
wingtips stretch beyond horizons
encircling the Great Mother

Roots plunge through feminine folds of receptivity....

Branches tipped with velvet green of impossible beauty
feel their way through our constellations
to solar systems in unimaginable galaxies

I lie among bugle, cowslips and dandelions
praying for deliverance

Mark Maddrell

A Covid Cure – April Wild Flower Recipe

First, *wash your hands,*
it's an absolute necessity.
Use a *disinfected bowl*
for best disease control.

Take a good scoop of confetti
– for sore lungs, try pink/white
spots of cherry. They are
light and always cheery.

To prevent a person dying,
add a pinch of dandelion, to
cool a rising temperature,
slip in a dainty primrose, one

grown in dappled shadow, or
try a dish of daisies to allay
the minor *symptoms, but*
if something stronger's

needed, try the essences of elder
– very tart! And beware
of holly for diseases
of the heart. Do not ignore

the *guidelines, keep your*
distance from the celandines.
Mix all ingredients well.
Bind in your healing spell.

Alison Lock

Perhaps answers are yeast

and rise very slowly

And Ever Ache

Dawn breaks unlike the human need to be touched. On wards, when hands don't shake, they fold. The same again tonight; making rubber gloves last. All wrapped in various plastics, a second skin that still my heart reverberates through. Shut the door between function and emotion.

Texting my mother on toilet breaks. Staff room full of buzzcuts and acquired germaphobia, a collective muffled voice. Scratching itches with elbows, everything with elbows. Fingerprints levelled from antibac, our affinity borne of mutual risk; of witness.

On the outside I am counter to visible society — bug of the open air. Picnic lovers and some buddies still gripping on to handlebars, in spite of it all. In public, hands don't shake, just applaud.

It's quickest to cut through the cemetery. The irony is not lost on me, in fact it's all I have to hold. Green gravestones and the urge to bleach.

I whistle bacteria through the streets at prescribed distance, my inadvertent imprint for the transient moment. Text my mother, rote jargon of acceptance or relief. I am aware that I am changed.

Furnishings bleed into a mirrored context; home consisting of hospital bed, hygiene apparatus, sluice. The frailty of lungs, essential role of courier. The absolute satire of desire amid disintegration.

Gorgeous knock of an ungloved fist.

The outline I've come to crave, unsevered from my own by movement of a hinge. She is standing about a foot away, helmet at her side. Other hand raised to just below the chin, as we've come to practice. I admire the naked palm. It is almost sensual.

Skin quietly clicks as our fingers interlace, thin membranes conversing. Clammy and undressed, like twin wounds. My hands never shake in yours, one of us says.

See you tomorrow, replies the other. She ungrips and turns, leaving at the threshold my online takeaway order and a feeling of vacancy. Us key workers, a commonality after all.

With similar embrace, I take the knotted bag to cot-side, recognising myself in the polythene. The strange heat of parallel experience; I am fed on its perpetuation.

Between duvets, hands just clasp each other, whisper something like prayer. There, there.

Remnants of consciousness segue into a fragmented yearning. When the impulse to turn things right has passed, where will we be?

The human need to be touched. In this way, I can reach it myself.

Peter Scalpello

Corona Coriolis

Bucket lists on hold,
both young and old
are being cheated of
their dreams by this.

Breaths are being held,
careers, relationships,
solvency for some,
escape for others.

All freeze-framed
as the threat rolls on.
Is there a precipice
to come, a mushroom cloud,
a whisper, or a bang?

"As flies to wanton boys…"
the mad king said.
As on and on
the virus spread.
Will that sigh be the last?

John Wright

Mask to Give Protection from Sorrow - Ama Bolton

Goodnight Buddha

For weeks now, words remain unwritten
the world too large, too small, both.

Instead I speak out my thanks, daily,
let the words out to float

and drift up the stairs, after the T.V. news
after the empathy of tears.

Pull back to the little saving moments.
I speak them out, as I step up, to sleep, or not.

This new world has leaked into my dreams.
I do what I can to mitigate.

So, I say goodnight to the Buddha
at the bottom of the stairwell,

say thank you to the silent smiling figure
tell him the triumphs of each day

how I helped Harry, Eden, Jay and Emily,
helped all fifteen of my locked down teens.

How my sugar snaps give deliciously,
grow tall in thanks for my support

how the latest peas have pushed up in pots
eager to hear my first words of praise

how my cosmos have started to bud
and none have been eaten

how I stretch, lean and balance
over the strawberries, twisting off

their green ruffs, eating as I pick,
taste sensational, fingers stained deep pink.

Buddha, the roses are glorious. Despite all the changes
the runners still know how to spiral up towards the sky.

Claire Grace Coleman

In My Frustration

I turn to Zentangles
armed with pastels, pencils, ink.
They tone down my anger to fuchsia.
They colour my frustration beige.

I turn to Woods and Water,
weird, forests and oceans.
They sing their secrets to me
on tree breezes.
They pull pebbles in their undertow
and drop them gently somewhere new.
Or they crash them to the cushion of the shore.
Always moving. The calm of motion.
The knowledge of water that can only flow.

I turn to puzzles.
Filling in letters and numbers.
Sudoku squares.
Using logic to name people and years.
Break codes to decipher sense.

I turn to patterns.
The certainty of circuit boards.
The tessellation of wall-paper.
The elegance of algebra.

Sarah L. Dixon

Long-Distance Massage

Since the virus forces us to stay apart
let's imagine an Ayurvedic massage
in Kerala's perfumed humidity:
two bonsai women
coiled in bright silk
spread us naked on wooden slabs
swamp our bodies with coconut oil
before cradling our heads
rolling them softly from side to side.

Now their fingers seek
neck and shoulder muscles;
the massage is vigorous -
we won't fall asleep
but we may slide off the table
like blubbery seals
in a shore-wave of oil.

The women bend over each limb
pinching fleshy arms
kneading joints in legs and hips
they press muscles into surrender,
then our bodies are squeezed
between soft palms
as if we are puff pastry -
let's inhale their sweet aroma of vanilla.

Now we are encouraged
to breathe deeply deeply
down down
into our stomachs.

I am invigorated
yet calm and released
How was it for you?

Margaret Eddershaw

Possessions

For Paul

There are items I want that are lost now: an old love letter,
a postcard, an embroidered Victorian case for stamps.

There are things I keep that I don't know what to do with,
and bits and pieces I think will come in useful one day.

There are things I cannot let go of: a green jumper,
a black rucksack, a jacket.

There are living mementoes of a past time like the
Christmas cactus I grew from a cutting of my mum's.

There are new treasures found at charity shops, eagerly
swept up and brought home.

There are things I never knew I loved until they were broken:
Dad's turkey plate, a teapot we bought
the day Matt went to China,

an old peg bag.

Susan Jane Sims

Belongings in Coronavirus Times

The flowers in the vase are so dehydrated looking
it's almost as if a big flower press
came into the lounge and took the light.

Coronavirus has shrivelled the outside
no playing in the parks or walking in the countryside
we queue, the social distancing in supermarkets.

If we are sick, we must not go outside at all
the sky is so blue, encouraging birds to perform
for you and I. Artistic dance - ballet dancers.

How stunning their feathers seem
isolate larger feathers from the smaller ones,
their colours: not a fudged brown or grey in a sky.

They seem so near, you can touch their tutus
an improvement, no planes and industry in the skyline.
And the ballet shoes are perfect with everything.

Johanna Boal

New Vocabulary

The curve
a graph that builds
reaches a frightening point
I ache for those who cannot say
goodbye

Lockdown
has no jailer
but is dinners alone
packs of cyclists around the lake
a siege

Covid
travels quickly,
creates fear .....my stomach's
acid rush with each announcement
panic

Screening
has no popcorn
no late night cinema
just an attempt to contain the
terror

Social
distancing a
line that measures love in
metres the space between feels like
torture

Pippa Hawkins

Filling Gaps

We have all fallen into a new routine,
feel a bit like casual workers stacking
shelves, or librarians returning books.

We might have a go at grouting tiles,
tutor ourselves on YouTube, or maybe
colour in those therapeutic patterns.

Whatever we do, it's only filling gaps
of our own making; just stepping over
the cracks that were starting to show.

We could try dentistry with amalgam
and end up botching things; *bite down
hard* we'd command, *have a good rinse.*

Pat Edwards

Diving

Isolation begets introspection. I learn that, like Whitman,
I contain multitudes, a thousand million pieces, none of them
the same. This memory of the wild rushing river closing over
my head, the cold treacle silence and dappled blue grey light,
before I surface, gasp; see the small boy on the hunt for cray-
fish with his red net. The sign reads *tents will be shifted*. The
stones get into my sandals as we walk back from the river's
edge. Finding those jagged edges, tongue diving and flicking
over sharp corners and lost fillings. Remember what I said
after I woke from anaesthesia, waffling on brightly bored
nurses about the brick built bunker in the back garden. It
really does exist, though I don't live there anymore. My
multitudes need multitudes; fire sparking at the smile of her,
the guffaw of you, the drunken debate on Gramsci over too
many pints of bitter, followed by falafel kebab and a wobble
up Kirkgate, just in time for the last train. I am a jigsaw
missing all my pieces. Every friend, each lover fills a different
edge. It's a time for writing, time for thinking; to fill the gaps.

Jem Henderson

Pigs and Ravines

The woman on the bus asks for pig & a slice of ham,
her daughter still sleeps soundly in her pram.
The woman takes her ham and slice of pig,
her daughter loves to dance while fast-asleep.
The woman dreams of food, no fat, no grease,
her daughter wakes to find she has no feet.
The driver of the bus, a patient man
drives slowly, slowly, into the ravine.

Chaucer Cameron

The Honey-Wagon

It's coming to it when
the highlight of your day is the
arrival of the honey-wagon.
'Close all the doors and
windows,' he says with
a certain urgency. 'And
bring in the washing.'

A tanker lumbers up the hill,
hissing and huffing. The
driver, a handsome young man
jumps out. 'Hello!' he yells,
uncoiling a long green hose
and thrusting it down the drain.
Nobody dares venture near.

'What a job!' I shudder. 'Well,
some poor bugger's got
to do it,' my man says. 'Only glad
it's not me.' Finished, the
honey-wagon chungers back to
base. We open windows, breathe
fresh mountain air.

That's what lockdown does -
makes the trivial important,
what's for supper, the weather,
a visit from the honey-wagon
meriting top priority, its
clearing of local cess-pits
a hot topic of conversation.

Moira Andrew

How the Corona Passed Over

My kids spent Corona Passover wandering like Arameans,
skipping upstairs and down, inside and out, playing the
goat, waving and blowing safe kisses at Gran
on social media.

My kids spent Corona Passover like a flock of lost sheep,
wagging their hands like the tails of spring lambs,
begging Bo Peep to find them.

Oh, my sons, my abandoned sons.
Oh, their new-born brother.
Oh, my darling girl.
Oh, my sons' absent mother!

Natalie Wood

Silence and Conversation

Silence and conversation; in the long day
These two come newly near.
Before, silence only happened in between
Other sounds, an unloved thing,
Unwanted but endured long enough
To cross the line.
Now silence, like sky, signs and surrounds each day.
Conversations? They happened but they were small.
Now, every word means more than it can bear;
Now, because we can't come close, much is unseen,
Everything that's said is precious like the wing
That lifts a bird into the silent skies.
Say what you mean, mean what you say - it's tough,
But fine, very fine,
In the saying and silence, to mean much, or all.

Michael Docker

Unlocking the Market

it's like a first rehearsal:
script unconfirmed
minimum props
actors uncertain of their roles
dubious about the cast
hiding behind masks
checking the space –

no gypsies flaunt gaudy garments
from the back of a shabby van
their colourful cries sorely missed,
each stall is socially distanced
holders' greetings are kind yet subdued
maybe to avoid arousing the enemy,
outstretched hands solemnly exchange
monster tomatoes for small coins

we duck and dive past masked women
laden with bags of dark green *horta,*
our purchases randomly bought
as though we are in a dream
or have forgotten how to choose;
we pounce on the first seasonal melon
like post-war children meeting a banana,
we clutch a bottle of olive oil
a talisman marking some semblance of normality
our bodies and minds unfurl reluctantly
in early summer's warm wind -
as we climb the steps to our house
I discover I am holding my breath.

Margaret Eddershaw

Kindergarten 2

3ʳᵈ June 2020

They have come out to play again
in soft summer rain. I hear their laughter;
the garden has been so silent.
I look through the trees
and pink dog-roses in the hedgerow,
to see them.

A-tishoo, a-tishoo, we all fall down.
I write again in my notebook.
Please God, keep them safe.

Denise Bennett

Dreams Delivered by Bike

In the absence of bread flour
that sounds appealing,
only how would I disinfect them?

The one about making love
to someone who no longer loves me,
the way he stroked my hair?

The one about supply teaching
totally naked and dying a death,
I want mi book, I want mi book!

The one about not getting to my dad
however hard I swim though he's dead
in case he's run out of something.

The one I only half remember,
just the feeling of being held
that stays with me till early afternoon.

I picture the delivery boy
with his pannier of nightmares
riding hell for leather to my door.

Carole Bromley

When Prayer Feels Unanswered

Perhaps we're not using the right vocabulary.
Perhaps we pray too much and the silence is weary.
Perhaps prayer kneels on leaves, weighs too heavily.
Perhaps it's a stencil of *once-we-were-happy*.
Perhaps prayer's a boomerang bouncing back
to someone more worthy. Perhaps it goes underground
looking for mercy. Perhaps prayer's banging its head
on a ruthless doorway. Perhaps it's a windmill
of lost tranquillity. Or a bridge that collapses in pity.
Perhaps prayer can't alter the body's story.
Perhaps it's not taking responsibility.
Perhaps saying a prayer is its own beauty.
Perhaps the reply is *not-this, not-this – neti-neti.*
Perhaps answers are yeast and rise very slowly.

Rosie Jackson

Something to do with love

Paper, Scissors, Stone

My son and I head out below this gem-blue sky,
the world we know made strange
now we've been rearranged by two metre spaces,
masks, forensic gloves. These streets
I didn't know I loved until they fell asleep.

We skim the empty subway, pass the taped off gym,
the boy flying ahead on his scooter –
we stop below a window where his feverish dad
stands waiting for a glimpse of him.
They raise their hands, play Paper, Scissors, Stone.
So close these two, apart. The shape their hands
like a bird, like a heart.

In the park, people walk or run, alone
or two by two around the lake.
Is something cleaner in the air? The sky more blue?
The geese, I'm sure, are louder,
chattering at the gate like it's Speaker's Corner.

At home, my phone's a pigeon carrier, smoke signal,
a raft to float me on these strange new waters.
All day, my yoga teachers appear on screen
and I could almost cry to see them – Iva,
Luana, Joaquin. We move through
sun salutations, live stream. When this is over,
will I be able to do the one leg crow? This,
of all the things, I want to know. When I see
there's twenty others watching, moving,
my heart springs open like a beak.
Lord, let me think in days, not weeks –

At 8, we stand and clap for the nurses.
Above and below me, whistles and horns.
My phone cheep cheeps to say
they're on their feet in Lewisham and Kentish Town
and Cardiff – all of us are clapping,
calling out into the dark.

Hannah Lowe

Something to Do with Love

Surveying the locked down map of my world –
windows opening to landscapes of uncertainty,
Time dances like a god in the changing light.
Dwelling in possibility I take nothing for granted,
accept life as it comes, not the way I want it.
Something to do with love, a prayer to protect
us from an innocent touch. As the death toll rises,
so does fear and courage – key workers keep carrying
on, laying bare the injustices of our world.
Knowing there is no going back, we hang on
with the furloughed, believing in blue skies, bird song,
and spring in the dreadful winter of our hearts.
Hope lives like a virus born with a message –
Life's a gift, a thing of beauty, cherish it.

Shanta Acharya

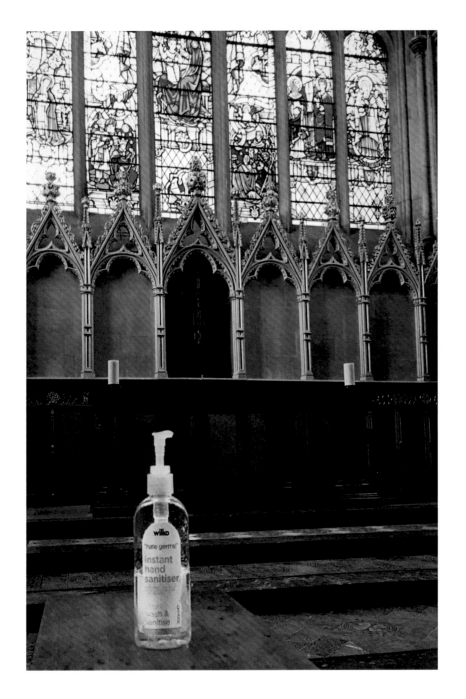

Instant Purification - Chris Sims

Teddy Bear Catches Fire at York Property

Left on top of a bedside lamp
the bear smouldered, causing a small fire
which was extinguished before three appliances arrived.

A little light relief from 2 more Covid 19 deaths in York
or updates on the Prime Minister
though I imagine its owner was traumatised.

You had a teddy which survived the dentist game
where you put the Anglepoise in its face
and then wandered outside to play football.

You were inseparable from it though its features
were burnt off, replaced by Elastoplast,
Will his nose and mouth be all better yet?

I think of you, wearing a mask and visor,
an apron that only reaches your knees,
ten thousand miles away in Canberra.

I can see the red marks it leaves on your face,
miss the familiar beard you had to shave,
as you tell me about your first Covid death

then change the subject and pick up
the banjo you borrowed from the anaesthetist
which you hope to master in your spare time.

I ring off and listen to Kim on Radio 4
watch a plane leave a smudged vapour trail.
Please take my love to Jonathan

Carole Bromley

Making Meaning

I'm trying to make meaning
To squash what little I know
Into neat round balls
To be stacked or bowled
Or put in the fruit bowl

I want to swallow it whole
Like a supplement at breakfast
Pour it into my bath with lavender
Take one in my coffee
Open it on my laptop

It comes in moments
When I'm attuned to my trust
That all is as it should be
But I lose it quickly in the grass

It scampers into the shrubs
The cat scares it off
Or brings it in twitching
Half dead, half alive
Meaning left on the kitchen floor

Lucie Meadows

Dusk

Grey skies pressing earthward
and earth chill, in lockdown,
an eerie absence of cars,
the few walkers harried by wind,
my own thoughts circling
on errands and shoulds,

then a side road makes
an opening, its rise drawing
my eyes upwards to fix
on a flurry of starlings,
a weaving of shapes
against rain-clouds,

first drawn out like a dark
thread, then puckering
to a circle, loosened again
and – higher, faster –
the delirium of follow-my-leader
sparking the sky:

my eyes and heart lifted,
the horizon suddenly larger –

Caroline Heaton

In This Less than Splendid Isolation

I would speculate right now
there are 78,000 Brits
starting that novel they were
always going to write
if only they had the time.

By my reckoning
1,600 will complete the job
and 0.2% of those will be stunners.

Perhaps now's the time
for me to give up on that fiction lark
and commit my myself
full time to poetry.

Connie Ramsey Bott

Weaving in Re-reading Eavan Boland in a Lockdown World 1
'No path back'

'I take down the book' after years of dust
read a poet layering her work
upon a marked lyric by another past.
'I come from an old' county.
'No path back to it'.

We were entrenched here once.
Now we are the strangers.
Outsiders.
Others find their ways along our river's overgrown but
established paths.
Others mark their deceased beloveds with living flowers.
Others fling open doors to let the children hullabaloo to school
or rather, did until
this latest fix
arrived like a rabid dog to spread through the pack then tear
to shreds our communal soul.

We have no way of forward seeing the way of the dark.

They had the Black Death, the dead carried in cartloads
from moor to mother church.
They had Leprosy, Typhoid, night vigils.
They had Smallpox, Cholera,
underlands of fear arriving in waves.
They even had Budd, the famous physician.
He told of super spreaders, C19 rule breakers,
like the servant girl who walked disease
to other villages, a chain of grief in tow.

If we could weave a way into the depths of their decrepitude,
if they could pull us back to know our fate, the facts of our
Age's chief destroyer
would we have the wisdom to listen, to comprehend resilience,
another century's survival path?

I return the book. Years,
& centuries snap shadows cowering inside.
The medieval Hall,
little clapper bridge over the Taw,
our ancient castle site, once moat
where we're told the poet reverentially picked her daffodils,
the Gothic yew,
moons mirroring in
our mystery Roman pool,
are rising
tolling bells startle the soaring sky,
our little Devon town
resurrects the disowned ghosts of its Atlantis past.

Julie Sampson

Reasons for Failure in Bread-Making
a found poem from Leith's Cookery Bible

If your yeast is stale or in any way insufficient,
you will find yourself left
with a poor rise.
One might also suspect
it's due to unsatisfactory kneading.

Cases of uneven texture
are a sure sign of too much liquid.
(It has been said in such instances
that the dough has not been knocked back enough,
but this is a private matter.)

Other issues arising in the failure
of your bread-making
will be a wrinkled crust,
sour flavours,
cracking.

It is important to remember
that if your tin is too small
or your oven too cool,
your bread
is sure to fail.

Zannah Kearns

What You Can't Have

I'm chalking up my domestic failures:
the sour-dough loaf, solid as concrete,
the mohair jersey, doll-size now
after its voyage through a hot wash,
the broken spout of your best teapot.
But oh, the sweetness of imperfection.
How dreary these days of lockdown would be
if I had cured myself of all clumsiness.
And oh! The fruit of the vine and the comforts
it bestows on my discombobulated spirits.
No, I don't know where your lost
green sock has got to – maybe the dog ate it?
And yes, it was me who finished the Chianti
while you were busy watering the cosmos—
You can't have your wife drunk and the bottle full.

Tessa Strickland

Twelve Weeks

I – 1620

Three months they sailed from Plymouth
toward horizons neither seen nor named—
terrified yet trusting for all twelve weeks—
an act of faith or folly absolute,
as hard to reckon, plumb, or understand
as the ocean deeps beneath their keel.

Once they could no longer smell the scent of home,
dropped in the pitch and swell of looming waves,
they heaved through seas like mountains,
now with only the scent of salt, the wash
of wave and drenching spray; or down between
the decks the stench of sickness and disease.

II – 1970

You made that journey, too, though not
by any means that asked for faith—
just Freddy's Sky trains plying back and forth
across the Atlantic's tangled loom…

landing all wide-eyed and ignorant,
flying into rippling stars and stripes,
sugared American apple pie…
yes, and motherhood—forever—

those first twelve weeks the coldest—
the days of your greenness—
the seasick days of carrying your child
in the ship of your womb with sails unfurling.

III – 2020

And now twelve weeks of isolation, lockdown
under contagion's decks—just long enough
to cross an ocean under wind and sail:
again without horizon: no landfall,
no astrolabe or timepiece as a guide;
no comprehension of the ocean's blues,

the wash of weariness, of sickness,
of waves of towering despair,
the tides of grief that roll & swell around us…
And yet, for some, twelve weeks of salt & suffering
to grow an unborn child—new hope through three full
moons—and more.

Lizzie Ballagher

Enclosure

You came a few days after burying grandma
propelled by good ideas and better intention
Yet to discover the power of letting go
you yearned to control each moment
Entered our cocoon for a month
Manifested worldwide enclosure
to extend your stay
Built steps to the land
castles in the air
Demanding in vain each day
to be the centre of my acentric world
Anger dissolving to guttural grief
only to be hauled up once more
from the ancestral well of invisibility

You are here
These wounds aren't yours
my darling boy
my greatest pain
my brightest mirror
my pride and joy
The Titans salute you
I salute you
who chose to be my son.

Mark Maddrell

Plagued

The air crackles with electronic noise.
Casualties rise, markets plummet.
Demagogues scoff.
Nothing to see here.
Just take it on the chin.
In supermarkets, people shove and scuffle.
We whistle in the dark, tell ourselves
Only one percent. The seas are rising.
In Africa, a plague of locusts.
Australia's ablaze.
I tell myself there have been plagues before
and the world's still turning. Still, this time
there seems to be a trailing off,
a slow silencing,
a dark finality.

Susan Castillo-Street

One Day

For Olly and Rebecca

At our father's funeral you played Bach, so gentle
Now the world, as it is, you can't pick up
your instrument and join in with other musicians.

There's a score of a song on the walls of your new house
and I hear the first notes to be played on your saxophone
which, for the moment, lies idle in the corner of a room.

It doesn't suit you not to play and make people happy.

You will have plenty of music in your house!
Your children are creating assault courses,
jungles, over and around old furniture, the settee

you once wanted to abandon, but plans seldom work.
Rebecca goes each day to the front line
and you worry. The children will need lunch

but outside there will be the smell of the lilac,
the garlic and the fox will slink across your lawn at night.
All of these things are music and we wait until we hear you.

And we will, again and again and again.

Wendy French

Clap for Carers

Leafy London street,
Genteel, Victorian, sedate.
Dusk has fallen.
All is silent, eerie.
Then we emerge, stand on front steps
Roars of applause ripple to sky.
People drum on rubbish bins,
bang on pans, smile and wave
across the street, nod to next door.

Though we are in isolation
I have never felt such closeness.

Susan Castillo–Street

The Masks

The masks we wore!
Oh yes, those masks!
The masks on our faces
Did not mean the virus won
To forever silence humanity!

Nor that it diminished our hopes
And our vision
One little bit
Our voices would louder
Instead, be heard;
Long after we were gone

Our battle's blood and sweat
The lonely tears
Shed like raindrops
Across the length of the globe
From the sidewalks of Wuhan
To the alleys of Vancouver

Would not water earth in vain
Rather we would emerge
From its deadly shadows
Stronger!
Triumphant over the mountain
Of our most novel fears

Sprouting like the good seed
From the sacrifice of one too many
Nameless public health heroes
Who came to the fore!
A wiser & united human race!

For the masks helped protect us
Gridlocked matrix of disease
In darkest of uncharted seas
Without hiding the soft beauty
Bravery of our humanness

Steven Mwalusi

Hanami Sakura

You email from Japan,
tell me you have ventured out
to view the cherry blossoms.

No picnics this year, no sunset
gatherings beneath paper lanterns.
People stand a little further apart.

The calligraphy teacher's daughter
has drawn you the character
for *sakura*, a flourish

of dark brush strokes
to hang on your wall.
You explain the meaning of *makai:*

flowers at their full weight of blooming
and *hana-akari:* the petal-light
that crowns each tree at dusk.

On our one-walk-a-day,
I lead the children past their school -
the silent playground, locked gates

the row of cherry trees
by the shelter where no buses wait.
The gutters are clogged with pink.

In both Halifax and Tokyo,
this is the time of *hana-chiru -*

Victoria Gatehouse

Note: hanami sakura is Japanese for 'cherry blossom viewing'

Sea View

Sails like butterflies tossed in violent seas:
storm-foamed waves churned from depths
by Neptune's fury.

Helios streams light through a sky break,
intensifying violet, mustard topped clouds;
illuminating a coast I might not see again.

Protected by glass, art survives.
Virtually waving through screens to humans I wonder
if turbulent seas will lose forever their butterfly sails.

Jenny Robb

This ekphrastic poem was inspired by Sea View by J. M. Turner, National Galleries of Scotland and written in lockdown.

Seagulls - Not in Isolation

Free to fly.
A life at ease.
You are my hope.
A memory of the sea.

No more wandering
along the beach. Oh no!
The cliff-top stroll.
Forgotten for now.

You cry, you squawk you chatter
on the roofs you call your home,
just as before. And yet, even more.
It's spring and, life demands life.

I can't see it. The sea.
I can't smell the spray.
But I hear it in your wing-beat
and I sense it in your flight.

No fish hangs from
those smart, yellow hooks.
Sharp eyes survey where is what,
from every town chimney pot.

Against the sky
I watch you chase.
You hunt and you are hunted.
Can you get your daily bread?
While I lull in choiceless solitude,
you have become my fortitude,
my solace and my hope. You are
my sea, my memory of freedom.

Sheila Gosling

Full of Covid-19

For Ewan on the Isle of Skye

The picture in the newspaper takes me to hills
where you're helping your parents with lambing
but you'd rather be with your new wife in the heat

and busyness of tuk-tuks, the frenzied way of Bangkok,
finishing your PhD, deciding on a future far from here.
Your parents too elderly to fly over mountains and oceans –

you travelled to them, the long, cold nights you had left.
And over the road from our house Clare sews gowns
for the most at risk in the front-line. Protective clothing

from Turkey held up on route. One particle is capable
of destroying lives. Meanwhile in the road children are
happy on bikes, one family at a time, out to play.

And your video has clicked in – the sea in the distance,
twin lambs just born, licked clean by their mother
and you are content to be as one, there, for now.

Wendy French

My Father

My way is a field close to my father
in the forest I meet my father whole again
completely human

At the start I thought love could stop you dying
with my help
with my input that day at the doctor's
with my help

My way is a field close to my father
but nothing I could do would save you from the fire
though I would have given anything

Talking to you has become a cape I hide in
if my words can become more than just printed objects
can soar and pierce the blue of the heavens

but my powers are limited, but they are earthbound
death took you from me and now you are sleeping
My way is a field close to my father

all my strength
completely human

Carole Bromley

Corona -Vorona Days -Ways

The humanity is caving in slow corona motion
I like a mouse back to my hide-hole,
Set an alarm every morn, lie in bed to ignore it
I stay, for what seems like minutes but becomes hours
Weeks and weeks in hibernation.

Sometimes I feel homesick in my home and
think I'm put in a home jail for not having corona,
It feels like a creepy clown chasing me
or I am being cornered by zombies,
I work from green home but the world is in red zone.

As I log on for socialising and switch on to remote voice
Are we all vectors or postcodes alike,
My body robots repeat eat, sleep and eat
Is breakfast still breakfast if I have it at 12 ?
Is dinner still dinner if I have cookies for tea?

Now this thing is non-fiction- health vs economy
The virus does not care
for the digits in your bank account
or your total assets or the GDP,
And even the fiction is dark, but there's still music.

The relentless race of traffic and people
have been turned into marathon conscious breath,
Shopping has became tracking down others health,
Sanitizer in the pockets, wearing face masks
Sneezing is a new way to attract attention,
Corona warriors on the front line,
but some people still curse and cry.

I blink my eyes, focusing in on the horizon
as if concentration itself will transport me to another place,
Did I just see a butterfly land in that flower?
When kookaburras cackle flying over empty streets
Do they know what is happening to us?
Am I noticing more than I did before?

The lungs feel clear, birds have replaced planes,
We venture out of the house to the garden and back in
again.
It's made all of us hermits
The sky is blue now, or is it just me?
Now I understand less means more.

Covid-19 is a hydra- headed challenger
to our modern modality to wake up
buying cheap tack from cheap labour,
I wonder why I feel a sense of guilt
when I see others suffering while I am not.
But I am now getting used to my pyjamas.

Sandeep Kumar Mishra

Wildfire

from many points of Mount Vesuvius
vast sheets of flame ... were blazing
Pliny the Younger

I wonder who will live and who has died.
My hair is burning ash; rock falls like rain.
This nightmare hurls my soul towards the tide:

the bulging cloud above our mountainside
is bound to smother homes that still remain.
I wonder who will live and who has died.

Infernos start to flare: I long to hide.
What shoots up in the cloud comes down again:
this nightmare hurls my soul towards the tide.

And where am I to go without a guide?
I choke on sulphur, mouthing my refrain:
I wonder who will live and who has died.

A piercing shriek rang out as children cried:
my neighbours must have suffered mortal pain.
This nightmare hurls my soul towards the tide.

The realms of land and sea may yet collide:
my world erupts with things I can't explain.
I wonder who will live and who has died:
this nightmare hurls my soul towards the tide.

Caroline Gill

Dorset Fields - Chris Sims

Each Day a New Bar

Each day a new bar that rises
and falls, a chart like the ones

half-remembered from school,
when you tried so hard

to crayon within the lines,
the columns a plotting out

of something inane
like favourite flavours of ice-cream.

Now struggling to teach
your own children the maths

(which has resulted in tears)
you deepen the desire path

across fields where summer grasses
slap like waves against your knees.

Here, the iron gates of a park -
the closed circle of a roundabout,

the climbing frame, cold-runged;
a playground deserted

but for two teens, cautiously
see-sawing, their conversation masked.

Victoria Gatehouse

A Plague of Flies - 4th April 2020

This first Saturday in April,
and fields, near and far,
have been laden with muck.
The stench that rears through
sunny gardens, through open doors
and windows, smells like death,
attracts a plague of flies.

Another plague which reeks of death
covers the land, attracting demons.
Some joke, some spool lists of intent,
of successes and some, unmoored from
steady anchors, beach on flats of fear.
Most make a meal of humdrum tasks,
like flies on their avalanche of shit.

Lesley Quayle

Corona Virus Diary

Sunday 12th April

Easter Sunday. I listen to the service by Justin Welby, the Arch-bishop of Canterbury which is being broadcast from his flat in London. His wife reads some of the responses. I am moved to tears… I don't know any mother who wouldn't be crying for her children this morning. Later, I phone my children. We keep the conversation light. I feel like I am acting in a play. I look at the pictures they have sent me on my phone.

Pictures

My son sends me a picture
of a simnel cake
he has baked this Easter –
that we cannot share.
My daughter sends me a scene
from her balcony
full of red tulips
that she has grown from seed.

I carry these images
in my heart.
The fluency of their fingers
more precious than prayer.

Monday 13th April

Flour is like gold dust at the moment.   A neighbour is searching for some so that she can teach her young son to make cakes. Blustery but sunny day. A friend has sent me a tonic – picture of some bluebells in her garden and a poem, *The Bluebells* by John

Masefield. Some worrying news from another friend who works with women who have been abused – because of lockdown, ten people were murdered as a result of domestic violence last week. Sometimes I feel like I am living in an Old Testament bible story.

Tuesday 14th April

Tom is doing some wood-carving, sculpting a bough from a tulip tree, into the head and shoulders of two lovers caught in a near kiss. The wood, taken from a fallen tree in a churchyard, was a gift from a friend. It's a beautiful piece. I like to think he is making it for our 45th wedding anniversary, which is in June. I am reading the poetry of the Irish poet Eva Bolan at present. It helps inspire my own work.

Wednesday 15th April

Yesterday Tom recorded me on video playing hopscotch in Havant Park. Someone had chalked a grid on the path, which I couldn't resist. He sent it to the children who said I might get arrested by the 'games police.' I can see the headline. 'Lady in a Yellow Hat goes for a Hop in the Park.' It was good exercise and great fun chucking a stone, hopping, straddling and balancing on one leg to retrieve it. I think I might set up a U3A group when lockdown is over.

Thursday 16th April

I sent out my first writing prompt to the Havelock Writing Group. We usually meet on a Thursday morning and as they were keen to carry on, I have set up an online course.
The first exercise is 'Fiction Squares.' Writers must select from different lists – a character, a trait, a conflict, a location and an object. Thought I'd join in so I have picked a waitress, young girl,

with pink hair who is short of money and takes a job in a tea-room to save up for some new clothes – maybe boots. Quick sprint down the Billy Line today. No hopscotch ! Shame.

Friday 17th April

First wet day for weeks. The gardens are dancing. Tom has managed to get us a 'click and collect' shop. Yippee! An outing in the car to Asda, two miles away, can't wait. I am doing my diary in a different place today. My neighbour has workmen in bashing up old crazy paving stones and laying new slabs to create a new patio, so I am in the spare room looking at a different view. I can see the top of Waitrose, my corner shop and beautiful feathery plumes of amethyst wisteria in another garden two doors down.
I clapped for 'Tinkerbell' again last night, tried not to cry …just mentally pulled the blinds down and went into mechanical mode, searched for the remote to find some more mindless telly.

Saturday 18th April

From my back bedroom I watch the comings and goings of parent blue tits feeding their young. They're a bit like us, foraging for food, trying to survive. I was pleased to see that the thee poems I submitted for the 'Nature Diary Project' done in conjunction with the national Trust, have been published on line. We continue to live in a bubble, safe in our homes only going out for a walk and occasionally for food. Wonder what will happen and when us oldies will be let out to play. I think of all those doctors and nurses on the front line but find small pleasures in my garden, my writing, in doing routine daily things, the laundry, cooking meals, the crossword.

Denise Bennett

Willow Pattern
a Lockdown Walk

Town's edge. A lane. A bridge. A field
marched by the battered stumps of maize,
lit by hills, broad as the moon.
The cracks in April clay will yield
rich oyster shells to feed poor days;
pipes; pigs' skulls; best, we find soon,

smashed pottery. And most is blue,
slipped from quick hands, a child's, a maid's,
to flags. Were harsh words spoken?
I brush a latticed rim, while you
scoop one white scrap whose two blue birds,
smudged lovers, soar unbroken.

Alison Brackenbury

In Victorian England, oysters were a cheap food.

The 'Willow pattern' on china depicts the story of two lovers, one rich, one poor. After death, the lovers are reunited as birds.

The Rapture

The Rapture will come.
In the Bible, it says.
A euphoric bliss.
But are we misled?

Has the rapture begun?
With me on my own.
Souls continue to perish.
But me all alone.

Alone in this dark room.
I silently pray.
Family and friends,
Getting snatched away.

O great cities of Earth.
O phantom towns.
Is this the Rapture?
Or Lockdown?

Mohammed Qasim

Lockdown Writings

12/4/20 (Easter Day)

This is the time of the birds.
Dinosaurs are still with us, and always will be.
They live their lives regardless.
Some beautiful, some menacing,
some comical, some clever,
all our feathered aliens hiding in plain sight.
Now I live with some
I am forced to confront their strangeness.

In this new quietness
the endless territorial battles
play out in song.
I am learning who is who,
another foreign language I can acquire
a surface knowledge of, along with
shapes, sizes, flight patterns.
Little by little, bird by flower,
I am learning to know Spring in our land.
The journey of a lifetime.

Jo Waterworth

Elegy for Easter 2020

Sparrows are nesting in the firethorn,
a woman round the corner struggles
to breathe through scarred lungs.
After four weeks, she's still grateful for her life.
Meanwhile, through the party wall,
next-door's bedsprings crescendo
as procreation's rhythm mounts.

A friend, sweaty from cycling,
delivers yoghurt to the side-door.
With gloved hand I take the pot,
leave it on the patio. Later, with gloved hand,
I'll put it in the fridge. With naked hand
I'll put out peanuts for the badger's treat.

Spring blossoms into Easter,
as the virus reaps a thousand lives a day
and on each station of the cross,
a chest rises, falls and rests–
the end of a twelve-hour shift.

Rachael Clyne

The Familiars in a Living Space

Not mad yet
I expect no answer
when I go to bed with Ted
and talk sweet nonsense

as I go up the stairs
I recite each night
what I found this day
in the way of gratitude

I think I should add a prayer
into the empty ether
for those who live in fear,
I live alone
I have no bruises
no broken bones.

Claire Grace Coleman

Hush Hush

Hush hush, sleep now
in this gutter world
where we find stars
like grit between our teeth.

It's luminous here,
where strip lights
and neon sicken our skin.

What of these bodies?

The curve and sliver of them
the cough and spittle of them,
we share so much.

My head throbs
the dim weight of skull
and it's clapper brain
clanging out crazy.

Wildness rats itself here,
slinks fox-like, penumbral
food hunting, between the bins.

Our tired street anatomy collectively
frightened by our next togetherness.

Hush now, sleep
form the grail of your heart
soon, we can clink our fragile glasses
share the light of ourselves
like rich wine.   **Susannah Violette**

Not Far from You

      in the garden
of a care home
      a stiff-jointed figure
in his best shirt and tie
      struggles,
with the help of his stick,
      to stand upright on
an old wooden bench,
        the better to gaze,
        grieving, through glass
          at his bedridden brother
        who has now stopped
          breathing.

Tessa Strickland

Daily Report

I woke to news of some government statistic
Or other, delivered by a talking head,
Words like 'model', 'line' and 'curve'
Were sprinkled through the brief report.

Is it just me who nearly goes ballistic
When they hear what's being said?
Just weeks ago our lives would swerve
Around such things, give not a moment's thought

To analysis like this. Fatalistic
Maybe, what with such numbers read
Each day; it doesn't serve
To dream of how we lived before we caught

This pandemic infection, this autistic
Interest in number straight out of bed.
Yet, what did we do to deserve
This? We lived & loved; sold and bought,

We did our best; meek and majestic,
Hoped and dreamed; low-born or high-bred,
Used and abused without reserve
And if we, unprepared, have come up short,

At least we lived; frail and fantastic
All at once and never once considered
That we might count the cost and have
To watch, straight out of bed, daily report.

Michael Docker

Calendar Kept in a Time of Crisis

APRIL

Wed. 1st   Soil and seedlings and the quiet flow of working
at will in a secluded garden!

Thu 2nd   Scent of garlic fronds growing wild in the wooded areas.

Fri 3rd   At sunrise the chimneys and treetops are lit with a golden
touch.

Sat 4th   Mare's tails in the morning, moon shadows at night.

Mon 5th   Seeds sown in late sunshine.

Tue 6th   Owl calls under a Supermoon.

Wed 7th   At midnight a corona surrounds the moon (it emerges
between the trees in the gap where I watch for it and lays
a bright path across my bed)

Thu 9th   The sun shines endlessly and hot.

Fri 10th   Seedlings emerge with tiny green shoots in shallow trays.

Sat 11th   Two blackbirds streak low over the garden at twilight.
Late at night a deep scent under bright stars.

Sun 12th   EASTER SUNDAY.

Woodpecker sound from the large tree below Balcony.
Walk on the Skyline but they remain out of sight .
(I try to use binoculars to find them)

Mon 13th   First signs of green from old potatoes planted three weeks ago in pots.

Tue 14th   Tender leaves at the topmost extremities of trees unfurl in the generous light of a gentle spring.

Wed 15th   Two crab-apple trees, in full blossoming splendour, one pale pink and one a darker hue.

Thu 16th   The golden light of evening casting warmth over all, the spiky crocosmia behind the little Buddha sculpture creating a kind of halo.

Fri. 17th   Lambs in large fields run to the ewes, butting at her teats; a family trio of cattle grazing.

Sat 18th   Soft gentle rain giving the plants a good long drink. (In Zulu it is called *kiza*.)

Sun 19th   The soft green on horse chestnut leaves backlit by sun. The wild garlic glints and white flower shoots emerge.

Mon 20th   The mellowness of spring days, where day flows into evening, and the gentle mood pervades all around.

Tues 21st   Light and Shade in Shepherd's Walk. Light at the end of the tunnel?

Wed 22nd   A small herd of cattle come through on the skyline, trampling the ground and being very skittish.

Thu 23rd   Clear blue skies and new seedlings showing in the warm sunshine.

Fri 24th   First potato shoot showing on Sue's allotment,
           where she's created a fine tilth.

Sat 25th   Glades full of flowering wild garlic at de Montalt
           wood area. A tall chimney remains from the old
           paper mill.

Sun 26th   Self-seeded plants tuck themselves into comfortable
           corners – and Nature takes its course.

Mon 27th   A day of muted light, all nature expanding, growing,
           exuberant.

Tue 28th   Rain a soft haze on green shoots, on leaves, on lawns.
           The birds still streak, the slugs still steal their way in.

Wed 29th   A green light on everything as the rain encourages
           growth and buds unfurl.

Thu 30th   A white froth on all the hawthorn now.

Verona Bass

Dispensing with the Rules

Once I was told what to make
with a lump of clay
my hands were guided
so that what I took home at the end of the day
was someone's idea of perfect.

My big sister used to hold my hand
so tight when she took me on ice,
that I never learnt to skate.

But this simple instrument
I'm holding now
is my soul singing.
No music to read, I play it
how I wish.
It's my therapy on dark days
a flute without rules.

Susan Jane Sims

*For the vine is a form of hope
rising from its root*

Hanging Out the Washing on Earth Day

With my right hand in a yellow Marigold glove, I delve into the pond, lift out handfuls of rotting leaves, twigs, detritus. Where is the frog-spawn? When I was small our pond was like a sea of jelly. Every spring I raised eight tadpoles in a tank. I watched them grow from full stops to commas, break out of their bubbles, turn into vigorous eating machines – don't overfeed them my mother says or they'll pop out of their skins – two of them did, too greedy for their own good; they push out hind legs, carry on swimming, until tiny arms with tiny hands appear. Before the tail falls off you must give them a shallow place to climb out onto; they need to leave the water, not forever, but to explore dry land, breathe dry air.

frog escapes the cat
leaps long-legged into pond
hides deep down in mud

This is a miracle, the coming out of water, adapting to dry land. Testimony to our own past, when once, like dolphins and seals, we too swam in the oceans and sang to one another. The pond has come to life. Snails have re-appeared, cluster in the shallows; some are spiralled, others cone-shaped. The lily displays small flat leaves on the surface. *Remember me?* she says. The water plantain puts out fresh leaves, promising "frog spoon" flowers; a pair of crested newts flick tails, flashing sunlight on their golden flanks.

water snails slide
upside down on meniscus
pond skaters make waves

I drew a portrait of a clothes peg this morning; it's a more complex device than you might think and more necessary than you realise.

How could you hang up sheets and pillow cases without a whole team of clothes pegs? Only now do those in power realise how indispensable are those least recognised of workers, the worst paid, the invisible: bin men, carers, bus drivers, shop assistants, ambulance teams, sewage works operators. All these and many others provide the clothes pegs of society, and have now been re-classified as Key Workers. The white sheet billows in the breeze, bright, graceful, laughing at the sunshine. This evening, the bed will be sweet with the sun's fragrance. My neighbour's drier rumbles on as usual.

a bootlace of snake
slips through a crack in the wall
tongue flicks in and out

Today is the fiftieth international Earth Day. What has been achieved in five decades? Perhaps we should celebrate Damage Limitation, and Awareness Raised. We wring our hands at the losses and imminent losses: the Angel of the Yangtze, the humble pangolin, the Northern White Rhino, the Right Whale, the diminished, beleaguered cod, Miss Waldren's Red Colobus. God knows, the list would be too long to write or to recite. A prayer of lamentation. Our own species is itself at risk, we know this now.

ants invade the house
wasp nest hums in the attic
woodworms munch oak beams.

Anne Boileau
April 2020

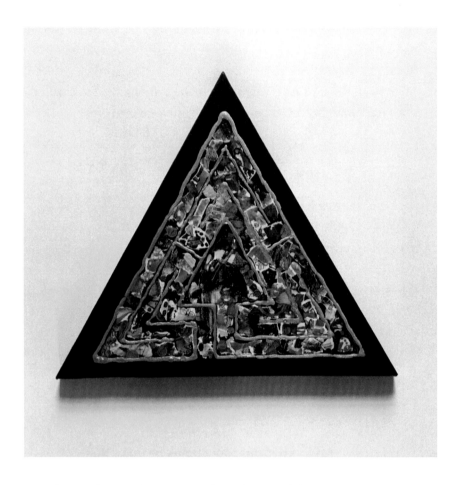

Labyrinth - Violet & Amethyst (Triangle) - Miranda Pender

Reading The Mirror & the Light

I'm travelling through this book,
meet sumptuous courtiers, creep
along the corridors, feel lingering
ghosts crouched in stone corners,
overhear its many plots. This spring,
any passer-by might be a carrier.
We queue for groceries, devour films,
clear garages – jittery as if plague
or sweating sickness were in season.

These people knew about mortality
- the rich fleeing to estates, the poor
fighting miasma with rue, angelica,
and prayer. I look out at my garden,
trimmer than it's ever been, filled
with Canterbury bells and peonies
others have left behind. The past gets
under fingernails; it never goes away
entirely. It's daring us to stare it out.

Carol Whitfield

WRAP
wellness recovery action plan

Flip charts spiralling bright catherine wheels
of mental health issues
as we share the air

as we inch toward agreement
as a functioning and self-governing group
about what it is we do

and it's mostly this —
while Sanjit Emily Jack and Marisha
flicker in and out of focus

to become useful illustrations
in this off-timetable late afternoon session
still we dither — most of us —

from detachment to wry scepticism
to engagement
achieving this much self-recognition

(along the spectrum of paradigm
and practice drawn
up by Tudor in nineteen-eighty-six)

she was diagnosed on a day such as this
before such an evening
it became the first in her slow recovery

since it's never things in themselves
that undo us
but our attitude towards those things

Martyn Crucefix

Chosen

You have been selected
to help relieve the burden
on the NHS by volunteering.
Having downloaded the Good Sam App
I decide to share my news.
Friends and family support
us the chosen few.
Would be Samaritans,
who must take our roles seriously,
and give greatly and generously,
through the gathering Corona storm.
There is no place for anything but calm.
Needing to still those waters, and rest assured
that God will ease the burden
on all of us, his children.

Carol Fenwick

Sparrow

In my old life a sparrow died in my letterbox

flew in and was trapped, her body desiccated in that summer's
heat and glued itself to a letter that said on the envelope:

"It died that was all. Birds die. How long do sparrows
  live anyway?"

That is a true story

This morning a sparrow conjured herself into my bedroom,
in my dream her wing beats were my heart as it fluttered
to wakefulness, they were her skirts as she, frantically fell from
the window like Alice down the rabbit hole. Then they became
wood splinters, spread like stiff fans, with her little body
gasping for outside.

This sparrow fell into the pocket of a bag like small change.
A pink and sparkly second-chance-at-life womb readied her
to find the sun again.

I midwifed her and as she perched on the edge
of her canvas precipice. From here she saw the sky, turned
to me without her wild-to-human flinch then flew away.

How long do sparrows live anyway?

Susannah Violette

Old Currents.

Too much coffee in the morning,
too much wine at night,
and the sky becomes fogged,
windows misted from the inside,
the phone silent.

The world outside is hard enough
to listen to. Its elements? Destruction
or living in the past; new gods demand
allegiance but I don't believe in prayer.
Wise-men bear only conflicts

and ordinary people, branded 'unclean' feel obliged
to hide themselves away until they leave no trace;
soundless and aching, they fade,
with the joy stolen from their hand-me-down smiles,
and no-one to claim them.

For now the sun shines, rooms are filled
with chalky light, the squares and parks,
the alleyways and tree-lined streets store
yellows, golds and acid greens, return the hope
of children, like salmon leaping against old currents.

Lesley Quayle

Colour, Not to Colour

It stands on the top shelf,
where I'd placed it at Lockdown.
I look at it, turn my back, walk away.
Not today, perhaps tomorrow, I think.
How long will this last, I ask myself.
Just another week surely, maybe two.
Not that fast, they say.
Six weeks, could be eight or ten.
No rush then.
My hair's in a state but I'll wait.
It trails my shoulder, brown black
below the woolly cap.
It's white at the hairline, parting even back.
Soon it will cover the entire dome,
perhaps to a stylish monochrome.
"Should I let it grow out, all white?
I ask him in the mirror?" It doesn't seem right,
"No one will recognise me".
"I will" he says with a cheeky smile,
"remember your......"
He stops mid air as I swivel round,
"That's funny, lucky you", I tell his back.
"You don't need the colour, you have no hair".

Leela Gautam

Lockdown Writings
26/4/20

Start the day by rubbing away at tarnish.
Find silver for the children.
It's always been there, beneath...

The grandmothers can teach us endurance
with their gap-toothed grins,
but you must work at it.

Every spring, plant and nurture.
Every summer, water your plants, feed your livestock.
Come Autumn we will be preserving sunlight.

The grandmothers know how.
This is only another disaster.
Love shines through –

It's always been there, beneath...

Jo Waterworth

I'm in Love with the World

I'm in love with the world.
The natural spirits move my soul.
I fly with the ravens,
Wriggle in the soil with worms and centipedes.
I swim in the living sea with fishes
And breathe in the prana
Freely available everywhere I am.

I feel more deeply by the day.
My heart expands ever further,
Drawing compassionate others
Closer into my trajectory.
The plants whisper and rustle-
Each a unique individual
In a group of souls.
I spend so long in the greenery
That I connect roots...
Leaves and branches
Onto my intuitive aerials,
And reach out deeper into the woodland.
Placing crystals, doubling the power
On energy lines.
I am tuning further in
Alongside another of the same soul.
The power is amplified again.

Ancient memories now begin to manifest.
Deep in my core.
I feel alive in every cell,
Every filament of my electrical being
Tingles with excitement,

For the great work
I have become immersed in,
Here on the beautiful blue and green planet,
Terra, that I have sometimes called home.
My future and past selves
Are here joined together.
Simultaneously reaching forwards and backwards
To my current incarnation.
A shiver down my spine
Confirms this to be truth.
I need no outside validation.

With sacred masculine beside me.
We complete a circuit, a quartz crystal-
An old yew on an energy node
Our subtle energies combine.
We heal the gridlines
And recharge what was forgotten,
Thought to have been long lost.

We journey together,
Home to awareness
Of our eternal selves.
For a few brief years in a lifetime already more than half over,
Yet connected to all that is
And has ever been.
All that we are....
A small part of the whole,
Stitched back together
Against the patchwork colours
Of earth and sky.

Julie King

Lockdown as a Kind of Pilgrimage

One day I will relive this as a time of elegy,
of quiet reckoning, try to recall the moat
of silence that circles the house, how chairs
and sofas have turned into islands,
the floor an ocean. My sacred journeys
in the world were noisier affairs,
no peace at all, the manic pace of India,
frantic rickshaw rides, poverty thrusting itself
into my face along with traffic, frangipani.
Now I'm watching through skylights as if this
is my meditation, the way clouds slowly drift,
collect, disperse, the way even the blue backdrop
is an illusion. Somewhere, presumably,
something is watching us with equal amazement,
equal awe, as we drift, collect, disperse.
How can a time of suffering feel so holy?
Surely we're being asked to go inwards,
go deeper, beyond shale and sandstone,
below hidden blocks and habit patterns
of our lives to the deepest source. Why else
are the usual sites of blessing closed –
Lourdes, Mecca, Jerusalem's holy sepulchre –
unless to remind us we must find love here,
in our cells of seclusion, or not find it anywhere.

Rosie Jackson

Bud

After Sean Hewitt

for the vine is a form of hope
rising from its root

upholding the spread of it.
for spring buds become summer candles.

for autumn's grapes bursting
to turn into the joy of wine.

for the garden where every flower
looks up to the sun.

for the rain that mother's the earth
nourishes its softening.

for the over-arching sky
its blue stillness, grey motion

the light of day, the dark of night
watching over every bud.

for every plant, bush and tree
living beings of green.

for even when invaders come
resist, hold on to the greenery of life.

Ruth Hanchett

Poppy in the Flowerbed - Alanna McIntyre

The Parlatorium, Orsova

A central no man's land contains a table,
the Austrian Quarantine Officer, and a guard
of soldiers; fixed bayonets, loaded firearms.

This market's in a wooden shed. Austrians,
Wallachians and Serbians assemble,
by realm, behind three breast high boards.

No mixing is allowed. Money falls from fingers
into a long-handled ladle an attendant offers,
then drops into a basin charged with vinegar

which is passed to the other side. Goods
must be washed or fumigated. Two yards
separate us all, but we gesticulate and roar.

Janet Sutherland

Details from: A handbook for travellers in Southern Germany; Being a guide to Bavaria, Austria, Tyrol (Etc) John Murray London 1837.

Russets

Coronavirus words:
isolation – distancing – testing
remind me of my childhood task
picking our apples
for winter hoarding.

Granny Smiths my favourite:
tough greenness resists parting
from the bowed maternal tree;
then checked for bruises
tiny maggot holes
the apple turning turning in my hands
hard and smooth as Dad's cricket ball.

Unblemished ones gathered in
for their lockdown in our loft
a cool dark space with wooden racks.
Each apple placed tenderly
stalk up like a small proud flag
an inch away from neighbours.
If they moved
touched another skin to skin
both would rot
and infect others.

Each week checking checking
for a tinge of brown,
diseased ones
thrown on the bonfire.

Once our cat invaded the loft
played ball with the russets –
always the most frail –
the whole batch burned quietly
like grannies and grandpas
surrendering to a virus.

Margaret Eddershaw

It is Unnaturally Quiet

in our tiny supermarket.
Some are locked outside
gazing in on a privileged few
stalking shelves.

Blue circles indicate
where we should stand
gripping our booty.

Checkout staff handle goods in gloves,
behind Perspex,
clean the surfaces
we touch, signal to
the next in line.

Outside we blink into the daylight,
conscious of twenty pairs of eyes,

watching, waiting.

Susan Jane Sims

I Am Not Sure I want to Play Games with No Clear Rules

Tidying the games cupboard.
Trying to find the red, wooden peg from my Nanna's solitaire
that has been replaced by a pen lid,
a piece of moulded Blutac or a marble.

I find the pop-die
from the centre
of a long-forgotten game of Frustration,
the cardboard edges mouldered away.

So, there are no longer
any squares to count out.
No zones or homes
where a pawn, tiddlywink
or metal-hat can be safe.
Free parking.

There is just a chance
of six random numbers
and a rookie move
sideways into games
where rules are lost
in dust, in a time before 8+.

Sarah L. Dixon

Self-Isolation

I am remembering the relief
of quiet things, my small garden a-tweet
with busy sparrow who join me to appreciate
leafy shade, a few tasty greenfly

while I read and doze and lose my place
in Chapter 17. The main road –
just a street away
but nearly silent for so many days
I almost forget it's there –

is barely a distant hum that rumbles
at the edge of hearing. Peace
and Wendy Cussons open up
heads like dinner plates, their petals
welcoming besotted bees who are dithering
between rose and honeysuckle,
backwards and forwards in a tizz of excitement.

It has been a lovely spring, full of blossom
and bloom and life, a big-hearted burst
of full-throated song from bluebells,
weeds, even silly slugs I've tried to persuade
away but who, what the heck, seem to like it here.

Such profusion makes me glad.
It's nice to see them back again,
yes, nice, a word Miss Regan told me not to use
and nowadays might seem to mock a world where
manic hype and overstatement
are required just to offer
proof of life.

I am sitting on my own
on my handkerchief of lawn
surrounded by simple flowers,
distanced from our old frenetic ways,
calmed by colour.

Shirley Wright

May 2020

Do not tell me these are gifts

the pure air
mocks the dissolving lungs

is charged with new poisons
dust of fear and grief
particles of rage that blight the ether

the blank blue
is the wall eye of a hungry demon

Do not tell me these are gifts

silence
speaks only absence
voices extinguished

sweet birdsong
a farewell to thousands

in the green flowering park
the slowly milling walkers trudge
weighted by unseen shackles
of the prison yard

they will not see freedom again
not as they knew it

Jane McLaughlin

3 ply

this darkest colour represents
those who have been extremely ill
and those who've died

another sober strand is full of fear,
either of catching the disease
or of too much loneliness to bear

but then, weaving through those
sober shades, there's a silver skein
of startling happiness

in people who are now enjoying
time to be at home, to be
together

who for the first time ever
can watch a bumble bee or listen
to a bird.

Maybe the rope of life has always
woven these threads in subtle harmony,
without our noticing.

Alwyn Marriage

The Long Bench

This poem is not writing itself;
it refuses to emerge -
the words are hiding out of reach and won't
make themselves available,
will not flow down my arms
onto my keyboard,
so instead as I rest,
I gaze through the window
at the blue sky peppered
with scudding clouds,
watch coal tits feast on peanuts,
note that the feeder needs refilling -
a job for later; and I listen,
as the string quartet by Dora Pejacevacic
drifts around the sitting room,
and I think how sad it was that she didn't live
to hear it performed but she
found time and energy
to create her manuscript,
despite her imminent demise,
and my attention goes to the wall,
where Kandinsky's Blue Mountain hangs,
and the Four Horsemen of the Apocalypse
ride with purpose to redeem us all.

Des Teufels liebstes Möbelstück ist die lange Bank.

Jane Hughes

Literal translation: "The devil's favourite piece of furniture is the long bench."

And Along with the Rest They Cancelled Football

Footballers become greater in the mind
the longer it is since they played.
George Best, he of the double-jointed ankles,
wove patterns between players so intricate
they might have been done with a needle and thread.

But he didn't forget the goalposts.
That's where the ball nestled,
home again, hence all the shouting.
With all the effort it took to put it there.
why take it out and start over again?

Because it's football, the game of the masses,
which also becomes greater
the longer it is since it played.

James Andrew

May

Language braided with ivy
    touches the streams of rain

Clouds thunder, swelled with the wind
They breathe heavily with the smell of forsythia and lilacs

The pond swings a silver fir tree

The time of sunny spaces is coming

Anna Maria Mickiewicz

London 2018

Quest

I used to dream I could fly,
spiral through the orange heat
of the sun. Mornings,
I'd misplaced the art.
Now, with books read deep
into the night, I flutter
on the draught of turning pages
in search of brightness behind
the window's dark pane.

My life hiding among pots and pans
and an airlock in the plumbing,
beckons. And in days that orbit
endlessly, in the unnoticed
ritual of cafetière and toast,
or hurried trek for bread past
a yellow glimpse of celandine,
I find the place where I meet
myself, where questions
that refuse to be tamed by sleep
are free to circle.

Yvonne Baker

Intimacy

In these days of distancing
I find ways that create
the illusion of intimacy
on my solitary rambles.

At the allotments I pass between plots,
sometimes on grass, or wood chip or planks
and I brush by the plants alongside,
not needing my two-metre gauge.

I stand and watch bees, three different types,
homing in to every welcoming calyx,
however small, for the nectar,
and I marvel at the close encounter.

When a friend brings flowers
I want to hug her, but instead we make do
with arms akimbo in a make-believe
embrace. Not quite virtual, but distant.

Verona Bass

St Mary's Church, Beaminster on VE Day, 2020 - Chris Sims

Calendar Kept in a Time of Crisis

MAY

Friday 1st   Wind whips the leaves mesmerically.

Sat 2nd   Two lambs stick their heads through the fence because the grass is greener there.

Sun 3rd   Potatoes on Sue's allotment are showing since their Easter planting – from my donation of sprouting ones!

Mon 4th   The Beechwoods bursting with wild garlic and white flowers fully out, a scent that has entered the senses.

Tues 5th   Blue ceanothus given as a gift to someone making a public space more beautiful. Plant was stolen and I gave mine as a substitute. Nice exchange.

Wed 6th   The golden sunlight on plants seen through a haze of tears. Clear skies all day and a full moon.

Thu 7th   A dreamy buttercup field and a hollow where cows have gone to lie down mid-morning, a warm day.

Fri 8th   V. E. Day memories of battle on land and on the sky – and we look at our clear blue skies at 11am to REMEMBER

Sat 9th   Bunting flags still hang in streets on a dreamily hot day. Everything feels suspended till 7pm Sunday and the Lockdown-Lifting talk.

Sun 10th   The wind increases, bringing cold air with it from the North Pole. Our Pole Star today is the PM's announcement as we wait for a lifting of Lockdown.

Mon 11th   Two little girls fly kites in a high wind on a wide open field.

Tues 12th   The slopes below the Skyline Walk undulate with strange hillocks, and are filled with buttercups and bugle plants. The May blossom everywhere.

Wed 13th   An avenue of trees on a sloping path create a tunnel of green with light shining brightly in dappled patches. (Just two months since I started this diary on March 13th)

Thurs 14th   Luminous colours in the garden seen through tears.

Fri 15th   Lengthening shadows on a large buttercup field where a herd of cows pass through, browsing beyond the stone wall.

Sat 16th   Potatoes in the allotments show frost damage, with brown shrivelled leaves, frost-nipped in the night.

Sun 17th   From cracks in the stone walls everywhere there are colourful protuberances of growth – valerian in pinks and reds, and there are small flowery growths.

Mon 18th   Wind whips the clouds into wisps of white and sends the trees in motion.

Tues 19th   A misty start to what becomes a sunny day. Birds swoop over the garden with a kind of wild abandon.

Wed.20th   A robin drinks from my pond, resting on a branch. I see it lifting its little beak.

Thu 21st   I walk in a field of buttercups and tread on clover patches, willy-nilly.

               May Bank Holiday Weekend.

Verona Bass

Lockdown Writings
10/5/20 .

The Government takes scientific advice.

The sun is too quiet.
It is surprisingly sleepy.
Some mammals are good at processing alcohol,
although not cows or elephants.
The dinosaurs have at last reconquered earth.
The air smells green.
With this machine we are gaining magical powers.
It's about life at the bottom.
There are only 128 possible values on the grid.

Jo Waterworth

(all sentences taken from current issue of NS)

A Tree Falls in the Woods

Hours sometimes spin into days and I seem barely there, in a dream almost, a bubble perhaps and then something can pull me up quickly, out of myself. Like today, when I was walking the woodland path, I saw one of the really large beech trees had fallen over, landed so heavy down the banking. There hadn't been much wind recently and the tree was strong, in its prime, still thriving. I was stunned, confused and I could only think that a giant had stamped on its base, held its foot there until the trunk broke into brutal shards, the exposed flesh of wood, hollowed. When I looked over it all, I felt such grieving, yet, I could see fresh leaves had sprung from its arms of youth. And now, even dead, it was reaching into the living undergrowth looking for a new situation.

Irene Watson

Bearings

You always wore that bracelet
zinc therapy you called it
a boost to the immune system.
It contained copper too
gleaming as you held my hand
on each evening trail through Culbin
forest, where several monoliths
recorded our DNA.
Tonight I feel the magnetic pull
of a gentle current
as I reach the tower alone.
With its dynamic view of the coast
I hear the bracelet whisper
this is how you survive loss
how you reach the other side.

Eileen Carney Hulme

Stay

if i told you about those times ….
"we camped like indoor strangers peeping through
blinds that cat had clawed cursing the living for
holding hands or laughing too loud
clapping each thursday counting at two each
afternoon grabbed what we could and stood
just how we should two metres apart and never
dared to cough
washed our hands till knuckles bled and bleached
anything that dared to move
prayed for a tory when he grew sick and watched
the old queen telling us to stay put
springs yellow arrived and departed while we
dreamt of lambs leaping on green hills and the
smell of the rape saw wasps try to sneak through
smallest gap and buzzard's climb on envied
wings as the sun rose and set on season and circle"

Andrew Scotson

Mindset

1.

What will we learn from this landscape?
The park gates shut, the promise
of trees and deathless skies

imprisoned within fashioned wrought
iron. Bars guard beds
where complacent tulips colour earth

extract succour from the croci's demise
the ornamental iris shrivelled
snowdrops that fail to show.

Captive outside the walls
we trail the perimeter hunched
in grey under the bitter light of security

to spite the day. We are lepers who seek
the intimate inner. Do not offer other
vistas, hills sweeping to sea etc.

They expose us
to unfocused abstractions.
We are indifferent. Resolved. Absolute.

******

2.

Hours gather in a corner, swarm
over wallpaper, cover camellias
someone—some unseen one

had printed to gladden drear days.
Now, as she watches they darken,
seep brown. She admits negligence:

leaves untended, his fallen blooms,
would have trodden them underfoot.
But these camellias, head-height,

smother, matt hair. Her brush
shushes a bud whose promise
is yet to flower. She cannot allow

propagation: grasps the cold shaft
of her steel comb, folds hand over
the infected area, holds breath. Pierces.

     ******

3.

When she walked, the hills gave her direction.
The north/south of her ungoverned thoughts
ignored the sun's contention of east/west

alliance. Pursuit of the sacramental
without collusion of church, murk of incense,
vestments, the priest's shrunk-conker cheeks

led her to where the Word lay, on the page
smeared, smudged, obliterated
by happenstance yet living.

When she sat she thought logic
resounded, yet still there remained
that other life, veracity beyond argument.

    ******

4.

In a shiver of uncertainty, of unknowing
where symmetry lies fretful and each
interlope of dusk, that larceny of light,
casts a truth for which we are unprepared,

we remain undefined. In the addled dark
the house merges with the hill, a raddle
of leaves ease the dulled election of sky.
A canticle from an unseen bird denotes

despair, sutures the edge of pain, arrests
the air where, penitent, we excise distress,
exclaim this our most precious possession
when only shadow lightens the impending day.

And here is the grief.
Here in this small house
in this small square where

light fleets each window
where absence is exalted
and songs of unseen birds

reside in untended trees.

Ruth O'Callaghan

Complications

Knife crime   statues   drone   GDP   modern day slavery

19

all this the surgeon hears before he shaves.

At work
he scoops out a shallow grave
in the cavity of the heart

a
gaping
gasping
eradication,

all
the while
his mind
circling;

those keys on the table, that note,
the roof of his mouth closing on her words.

Jacqueline Haskell

Fill Your Time with Purpose

Indoors, long term, is time for something new —
create, get thin, get healthy, so they say.
Advice is everywhere so must be true.

For all of us, him, her and me and you
the pressure's building each and every day.
Indoors, long term, is time for something new

with massive choice — what, why and how and who,
and we must buckle down or rue the day.
Advice is everywhere so must be true.

A million ways for us to see this through
forced down our throats in each and every way.
Indoors, long term, is time for something new,

ideas and interests that we should pursue.
It worries me and fills me with dismay
that resting, thinking time has no value.

I want to shout I don't need things to do!
I can and will ignore it when they say
indoors, long term, is time for something new,
advice is everywhere so must be true.

Denni Turp

Rapunzel

I never thought of all that time
alone in your tower
with nothing to do
but watch your golden hair grow.
How did you wash it?
How did you brush it, braid it?
You, punished because your father
stole some herbs? You,
just twelve years old?
And the kind prince
who saved you
(it's always a prince),
was he really kind?
Or were you just so relieved
to not be on your own?
Rapunzel, dear girl, I have
so many questions for you
now that your dilemma
somehow feels real to me.

Connie Ramsey Bott

Stained Glass inspired by Bath Abbey - Beverley Ferguson

Lockdown Walks

I gaze at far horizons,
almost weeping at their inaccessibility.
Rolling hills,
one with a white horse cut into its hillside,
distant woods, towns, villages,
all faintly visible in a heat haze,
but calling, calling!
Great flocks of sheep graze
across the sun bathed fields,
but there are no signs of life
in the nearby locked down hamlet.

A dead tree points jagged leafless branches
into the blue sky.
It has been dead for years
But still marks the countryside with its presence.
If I die at the end of all this
I will leave no trace here,
Just memories.

The subtle colours,
greens and browns and sheepswool white
massage my aching heart.
Will this ever be over?
Will I ever walk again,
freely,
to those distant hills?

Andrew Lawrence

Blue

It was the blue summer.
The sky cloudless,
unmarked by vapour trails;
the delphinium I'd always wanted
flourishing in my newly planted border;
the Buchanan tartan of the picnic rug
spread across the parched grass.
And racing up the hill each evening,
light seeping through closed curtains,
the pulse of ambulance beacons.

Angi Holden

Groundsman

I love the way he drives a five-gang mower
over this fanciful course, side cutters bouncing.

He cuts magnificent stripes all along the fairway,
swathes of green, stroked north, stroked south

and now he slaloms playfully round avenues
of lime, cherry, chestnut, willow, birch,

pirouetting round their untouched trunks,
spreading ripples in the grass.

Don't talk to me of weed killer, fertiliser, fuel.
We need somewhere safe and beautiful to hide.

Sarah Mnatzaganian

View from the Rough

The water hazard's far too full of weed,
but still the willows fling their long green hair
like Monet girls, down to the dirty lake.

The cherries are so white they startle me.
I'd pick their brittle twigs and take them home,
if it wasn't blasphemy.

Now we've just one hour a day outside,
I'll take my time in this managed paradise.
Stay in the dew-drenched rough.

Wave long and gratefully to the groundsman
practising his calligraphy
around the wakening trees.

Sarah Mnatzaganian

Fantasy in Blue

The good looking man of a suitable age
in the adjacent queue in Sainsbury's
(also carrying a singleton's basket)

laughs at my effort-noise
and asks *Is that your workout?*
as I heft my basket up

plonk the bottle carrier down.
I flash a smile back, reply
Yes, this and watering cans.

In our blue gloves we unpack
pack, pay. We have paid, paid
and paid; in dismay at the relentless facts,

in distress at the haunting stories of others,
in knowing the price of isolation for ourselves.
We are so in debt we are rash with it.

Don't be a stranger, hold me.
We link burdened arms
and hurry to his car, which is closer,

throw purchases in the boot.
We open doors, rush ourselves in
kiss and kiss and kiss. It's bliss.

Claire Grace Coleman

Somehow whenever the music

stops

it's Wednesday

Less Being More

Now that the past has been eaten by moths,
the future fallen like seeds in a forest fire,
I seek refuge in the present, though it's unfamiliar,
as if I too am drifting between worlds,
caught up with thousands of souls unmoored
and bewildered by their unexpected death.
I too struggle to become other than I was,
I too lost for words in this vast homecoming.
When I turn to poets for help, Jack Gilbert,
who knew all about beds and bodies,
human love and its unmaking, offers me titles
like 'How to Love the Dead', 'Cherishing What Isn't'.
He encourages my use of unfashionable language,
heft, tenderly, meanwhile, marred, tells me the eight years
since his passing have stretched into the no-time
of legend, less exile than living in a land you know
you don't quite deserve, like his sojourn in Greece,
that perpetual wonder of islands sleeping in the sea,
sand almost too hot to walk on with bare feet.
And yes, he says, it's fine to improvise,
imitate his best lines, *'the ruthless furnace of this world,'*
'Mortality like a cello inside him',
he's beyond attachment to any of his darlings.

Rosie Jackson

Lament

For my cousin Helena who died 7 May 2020

We soften the face of death with flowers and verses
and *we'll meet again* and *I'm only in the next room.*
We will not meet again. No-one is in the next room.
You are further away with each day that passes.

We die as fish thrown on deck to drown in air
as hens on the conveyor hanging by their feet
as fox in a trap or crow nailed to a tree
as sheep felled by captive bolt or rabbit in a snare.

Daily without a thought we take their lives.
Our lives are worth no more or less. No god watches
over you or me or the hawk or the sparrow it catches
or the flea or the fly or the virus that survives —

survives one death after another and will perhaps inherit
this plundered poisoned world and all that is in it.

Ama Bolton

Pain

strikes without warning like a professional assassin,
working with exaggerated slowness and precision,
plays a game of cat-and-mouse, leaves me
stunned in a tangle of nerves, sucking the energy
out of me, flicks my days like images on a screen –
menacing lions ready to drag me into oblivion
when the jungle morphs with flashes of lightning,
and I begin to see things I'd never seen –
past and future unfurling in ways unimagined,
my days measured in blister packs of agony.
Lying under the duvet, curtains drawn, I marvel
at shafts of light that lean in like angels of mercy.
For a brief moment dust appears luminescent,
glows like fireflies dancing in the light.

Shanta Acharya

Some Trees

An ash-tree in the fierce glow
of sunset out beyond Heathrow
    seems all ablaze in every leaf –
        and gazing feels a form of grief.

Horse-chestnut with a brittle crown
of summergreen pricked out with brown
    seems all ablaze in every leaf –
        and gazing feels a form of grief.

An elm-tree I remember there
as hardly more than twigs and air
    seems all ablaze in every leaf –
        and gazing feels a form of grief.

Toby Litt

Company of Trees

Each poplar, lime, ash, oak, says
my people are not far away,

They're close enough for a bird
to sing from one, be heard by all,

close enough for roots to meet, talk,
feed each other, warn of disease.

Come, everyone I love! I'll watch your faces
change with every day of spring.

Feel on my skin the same roar of rain
in your listening branches.

Old man willow will grow new arms
from his sawn trunk.

Birches will shed silver without pain
and caterpillar the grass with catkins.

Black barked cherries will unleash flowers
of white, then rain-crushed pink.

In any other spring, I would have stolen
your undefended blossom.

This year I need to see your canopies
triumphant, complete.

Sarah Mnatzaganian

Outside Sainsbury's

I shuffle along like a sheep
not thinking much more
than following others
obeying the lines and the fences.

A cough comes from someone.
We each pay attention
just for a moment
then resume our linear progress

gradually shifting the weight
in a sort of a walk
without any question
preserving the distance between us

moving forwards with not much to say.
New followers join
the straggling line.
Spaced out on this well-trodden track

together we make up a flock
on its way to find food
each wanting the same
through the gate that is open ahead.

Richard Westcott

The Summer of 2020

Covid 19 holds us all to ransom
in our homes for weeks, rainbows
posted in all the windows along the street.
Over the world, race riots turn ugly.

You tell me you have found another
doll's house to restore. I marvel
at your find. Great crested newts
thrive in the pond nearby. The crab apple
stands taller and bushier than before,
young fruit already peeping through
bright green leaves.

I dream of bales of wool again,
descending towards me, threatening
extinction. The garden flourishes,
reviving hope; the first flush of roses,
the brilliance of geraniums in mauve,
and pink and variegated peach.

I breathe more easily today in the cool
air, after days of blazing sunshine.

A postcard of the Abbey falls on the mat.

Anna Avebury

Watching Countdown: Wendy Halsted

Directions

Tell the family
they can't all come.

Collect the body
from the morgue.

Safety is imperative:
follow guidelines

when handling
Covid 19 corpses.

Take the coffin
to the crematorium

Then return
for the next.

Space of course
is running out

but keep up
a good pace

and put on
a good face,

added the
funeral director.

Ruth Hanchett

Beach Walking During Lockdown

What I have enjoyed is my low tide
beach walks with my buddy Jill.

We check the tide tables every day,
and know to meet 15 minutes early

with our boots on, and then we
walk and talk, praise the sky,

try and decide what colour the sea
is today, admire the unique patterns

on the wet sand every day, look out
for unusual shells, wonder how

a scattering of broken or half-eaten
crabs sometimes arrives here,

enjoy the dogs etching patterns into
the sand, or skipping through the waves,

and remind ourselves that there is
so much about the sea we can never

know or truly understand, and this
is something we will carry on doing

after Lockdown, something to look
forward to, and structure our lives around.

Brian Docherty

Silence in the Time of COVID

Silence is only the absence
of familiar noise. It has its own sound.
The warning beeps
at the level crossing announce
the barrier coming down.
An empty ghost train rattles by
full of empty seats and yellow signs.

I hear the birds chattering to us
from the trees.
The tide is out, the beach quiet.
Occasional gulls.
A few odd walkers.
Abandoned sand castles.
The smell of summers past
and pairs of children
playing separate games.

A game of "I Spy" on an empty beach
fast fails due to lack of inspiration.
Twenty questions
ends
on the perfect pitch note
of my child's peals of laughter
fading into the sand.

The Blue Sky, punctuated by clouds
and threatened rain,
reveals a small arc of rainbow

rising out of the old lighthouse.
It ends before it has scarce begun.
Violet shimmers at the edge,
red into orange on the other side,
disintegrates, then
begins again.

One day we will look back in wonder,
and tell the stories of how
for just one short moment
our world stopped in its tracks
and there was awe and wonder in it all.

Aoife Doyle

Empathy

Sometimes I lie awake at night
and remember all your faces
The smiles, the laughs, the tears, the 'fight'
You're my people, not just cases.

You walk into my clinic room
with mingled hope and fear
Due to Covid we may meet on 'Zoom'
but the feelings are still clear.

There are countless happy smiles and tears
'Your scans are fine', I say
My heart is light, I calm your fears
and seize the blessed day.

But sometimes I fail, (no fault of mine)
and bear that helpless feeling
As I walk the ever-thinning line
between empathy and grieving....

Rema Jyothirmayi

Reporting to Duty
(a tribute to my Grandfather, Ted Smith)

Creaking bones and the telephone are the order of business.
Meeting commenced at o eight hundred hours.
Curtain swiped; table readied.
Awake the sleeping soldier and
have him report to duty.
Do tread with care as
this life was built for yesterday.

Legs straight and arms askew,
crinkled sheets and breakfast due.
Fingers unfurling from the decades' rust.
All present and correct, sir.
Here lies a Yorkshireman.
Stiff oppa lip,
but of the kindest variety.

Succumbing to the years,
a body like a well used sheaf revealing the hidden blade.
Do not mistake this diminutive man as weak,
For deep inside there is a thrashing heart,
And a soul which sings for thee.
Arise good soldier, arise!

Alex Smith

The Storyteller

His cheeks are sunken now. Not through age alone. Illness and stress have played their part. But when he smiles… then you see his real face. And smile he does often; he's that sort of guy.

His joy is the life he lives here, in a Cumbrian lakeside cottage, with his darling Norah. His great sadness, the turning of his daughter's back for the crime of falling in love.

His wife died of cancer five years ago. Eighteen months later he met Norah. And that was that… tears and tantrums. "She's not Mum, Dad. Never will be. And so long as you're associating with her…"

Eventually she relented, just a bit, seeing how her twin eight-year-olds were missing their grandad and his whacky tales. Baz loved the monsters; Gav, the spaceships. But his only permitted contact was a monthly visit. These meant so much, the long drive worth every mile.

Thanks to the pandemic, his last time was nearly three months ago. And he sighs remembering Gav's wave: "See you next time, Grandad."

Yes, next time…

His cheeks are sunken when a miracle occurs. A kind text from his daughter. And minutes later, Baz, bubbly on the phone. Now Gav as well. Next time over, he'll tell them about a spaceship with monsters on board.

big band tunes
from the war
cooking smells waft

Paul Beech

Two Months and Counting

My body is close as close can be
the great holm oak's fissured trunk
is not comfortable to hug
to press with an urgency
born of need to touch.
Old bark dust stains clothes
my face is marked by creases.
I breathe in. I breathe out.
I breathe in its endurance
until I can walk on.

Claire Grace Coleman

Lockdown Ouch

I am ready
to give up.
It's simple,
I've had enough.
I care,
of course I do,
but do you, do you,
do you?

and if you do,
how would I know
know that you do,
how would you show
that you do,
you do?

I suppose if I knew
I wouldn't ask you
ask you who,
in my case, is off my case.
Who?
You?

Pru Kitching

End of Isolation

She's had it with the walls,

the towers, the space of flowers.

the mirror and the loom.

She's left the lot.

She's got

an outboard motor for *Shalott*.

She's off – zoom – "Lancelot -

fancy a spot

of tirra lirra by the river?"

"Sure babe, why not?"

Kate Pursglove

Kinsale - County Cork

We drove past Charles Fort
moon-wrapped and shadowed.

Descending into the cove
I stood gazing across the sea

a sea so still I thought it might be remembering
when I fished with my father.

'We are rowing near the Lusitania,' he said.
And told me the sad and dreadful tale,

he told me about the Spanish Armada, wrecked,
and fallen apart, how some survivors intermarried.

I pictured dark-eyed colleens wearing The Kinsale Cloak.

Snapping a photograph I returned to the car.
My heart a storm of memories.

Maureen Weldon

Black Lives Matter

Brought to the West,
Shackled and sold on a platter.
Let us tell the world,
Black Lives Matter.
Martin and Malcolm,
Bullets leaving their body in splatter,
Because they told the world,
Black Lives Matter.

Performers painting their faces.
For fun and satire.
Why weren't they taught?
Black Lives Matter.
And that beautiful black queen.
Racists shouting slurs right at her.
But she needs to know.
Black Lives Matter.

'We'll make a change'
Our governments did chatter,
But nothing will change unless we tell them.
Black Lives Matter.
And still we march.
Still mad as a hatter.
Why won't any one listen?
Black Lives Matter.

When will change come?
The people demand an answer.
When will the world see?
That BLACK LIVES MATTER!

Mohammed Qasim

The Nowhere People

*Dedicated to the migrant labourers who built India, but paid the
highest price for Lockdown and the survival of the richest*

Here they are:
steely-eyed men and women,
rust settling on
the iron of their skins;
slurry and spent fuel
steaming off their bodies;
road tailors sewing tattered beltways
with tar-mix and stone
for sleek Citroens and Saabs
to glide over;
deft workmen, fingers
texturing the terracotta,
trowelling walls
in rare blues and yellows
and whatever-else-Madam-would-like
for her three-tiered, fancy-cake-house.
Husbands, wives, and distant cousins,
sutured-together bodies, souls and minds,
coming up for air every evening,
ghosting through the nights
around fires fed with plastic;
making frantic love,
re-hanging stars in the skies above
the coolie lines of cities.

Then Lockdown clamps jaws
over nations, lives, livelihoods;
grinds wheels, cogs, and pistons
to a halt;

grinds machine-made men and women
to slag;
leaves a glimmer of survival
in the few who wait
for buses, boats and last lorries.
Imploding men
keep lamp-lit vigil
over barely breathing babies,
or sling them over cycle bars
and make for the pumpkin fields of home.
Highways crawl with migrant life
caught in the final flicker:
mouths closing, opening, closing.

Think of dark matter in a coalmine;
think of a train, a dysenteric cubicle, a bench,
and death somewhere in-between.

Geralyn Pinto

Lockdown Sally

smells rather than sees the people around her:
pacing, skipping, eating cookouts, hanging over windowsills. Sweating.

One evening she even joins them out front – *Oh how she'll lust*
after that night! – and gets to watch musicians play, symbols chimed.

But outside is still the language of the enemy: hostile, impenetrable.

Since childhood, wolves haunt the wide plains of her memory,
as she cowers, exposed, under an old, grey moon.

When another Sally moves in next door, neighbours take to calling her
Lockdown, just so they'll know who's who, they say, no offence intended.

Loose rivulets of sunshine streak hair held back with yesterday's
bandana, in preparation for next time.

She tells herself – and them – that she'll go back outside again, soon.
But she never does.

Jacqueline Haskell

Hold

Across the back gardens a woman folds herself
now summer has come the green trees take her
and she   in her interior   shifts like a tree in a breeze
at this distance and behind glass she appears to falter

It seems she may fall   go down in slow motion
and I remember   the man in the late-night supermarket
whose back bent like the hill I can see from this window
 It looked impossible he could keep standing

As if through a dense fog   as if seen through a long tunnel
he sank to the floor without resistance   he
who would not rise again   seemed to be sinking
into a universe   where agency could be surrendered

Janet Sutherland

Revolution

On the first day, we toppled statues and threw them in the river.
On the second, we daubed slogans on insensitive monuments to the indefensible dead.
On the third day, we shouted down dissenters on Twitter.
On the fourth, we accepted – grudgingly - apologies from errant comedians.
On the fifth day, we censored old TV programmes, whose sentiments we reviled.
On the sixth, we burned the books that angered us.
On the seventh day, we demanded resignations from politicians who obstructed our glorious revolution.
On the eighth, we stormed the Parliament and dragged the government away in chains.
On the ninth day, the executions began.
On the 10th, we issued edicts to the media.
On the 11th day, we called on children to denounce the thought crimes of their parents.
On the 12th, we dispossessed the privileged, redistributing wealth to our heroic freedom fighters.
On the 13th day, we issued ration books to party members and forbad all others to buy or sell.
On the 14th, we declared a national holiday and erected statues to commemorate our glorious leaders.

Michael Forester

Full of Woe

Since March, there's been much to worry about
but I have mostly worried about Wednesdays.
There's more of them than is usual
in an ordinary seven-day week –
or so I have found.

There's Monday, that unlikeable day,
but no sooner is it done than it's Wednesday
again. There might be Sunday, bloody, Sunday,
but, quick-as-a-blink, it's Wednesday again.
Sometimes there might be a Tuesday,

that good news day, but that's always followed
by Wednesday anyway, then quick-as-a-flash
go Thursday, Friday, and Saturday,
and it's Wednesday again.
Some weeks go waltz-time

slow, slow, quick, quick slow
but somehow whenever the music stops
it's Wednesday

Marilyn Francis

In May 2020, Some Nights Are Still Frosty

i.m. Pat

It's not quite warm –
not even enough to be called *fresh.*

I stand at the top of the metal stairs,
lean at the back door. I'm on a level

with second floors, can see
over long gardens to the next street.

Windows blink back the sunrise
A jogger covers twice as far

twice as fast. There's no one else
on the pavement at this hour.

My lined jacket is knotted
over the railings, in quarantine

these last forty-eight hours.
(Fabric holds all droplets too close.)

It's cold and stiff to unloop
after a night of frost, like it's had a dose

of *Robin* starch. I think of what
you would've said – *warm it on the radiator*

then come and meet me for tea
and a Danish. My treat.

Alison Campbell

Paradise Bird

On the road past Ann Hathaway's house
there is a girl, about 9 or 10
in orange and yellow leotard
standing on one leg,
the other raised to her head,
a ballet position.

An older woman
in red skirt, gold t shirt, takes a picture
with a fierce looking camera.
The girl wobbles as I pass.
The woman says,
try again and the girl does.

The stillness in her body holds time
for those few seconds.
A bird of paradise.
Watching her I forget
about the fear sliding in my mind.
For this is a flag of courage

to take home with me,
to hold close.

Catherine Whittaker

Lockdown Writings

30/5/20

The best time to plant roses
is probably not at the end of the driest spring on record
three months into a pandemic.

The all-knowing search engine recommends
autumn, or late winter to early spring.
It's best not to plant them when the ground is frozen.

The best time to dream of roses
is probably at the end of the driest spring on record
three months into a pandemic
while sitting in your garden with a dear friend,
socially distancing,
listening to birdsong and bees.

The best time to buy a trellis arch
and a climbing scented rose
could be just before the summer solstice,
to celebrate your sixtieth birthday.

Jo Waterworth

Last Summer We Watched

coal tits build their nest in our box, painted pale
with slated roof, small round port hole.

We watched them dart and dash, pause, poised
in the busy-leafed damson, mouths full, some-

times both adults squeezed, crowded inside our box.
One morning we watched as one by one, each fledge

teetered on the mouth, paused, fluttered to the damson,
waited, waited and flew. This spring our garden is a-flush

with tits so we wait and watch our box painted pale.
We pause poised for them to give life to us again.

Marg Roberts

Bewildering Times

We find ourselves in plague time,
a negotiation between strength and despair.
Clear sky, sun over a stilled people,
alleyways of blossom, spring arrives quietly.

We are within boundaries, not going far.
There is fear, oh there is fear, that jumps and grows.
Panic makes eyes shine wild. But the birds
still nest, move spring along.

I write to my friend, due to birth soon: safe passage,
calm allowing, what an adventure my dears.
To another, cocooned in loss, stooped
under the weight of grief. Love.

A girl makes tissue rainbows, sticks them on the window.
She stands outside reaches up, smiles.
She and her rainbows glow in the sun,
Iris, small goddess, brings hope.

Rose Cook

An Alphabet of Things I Miss

Adventures on trains. Adrenaline. Anticipation.
Browsing in chemists, bookshops, stationers.
Cinema trips. Cafe chatter.
Dancing wildly with friends, not alone.
Evenings connecting over a pint or two.
Fussing dogs. Flirting.
Going on dates. Going on long walks away.
Hugs.
Inviting friends over for food and games.
Joking playfully teasing and being teased.
Kissing, snogging, contact.
Laughing hysterically with extended family.
Making new friends. Museums.
Neighbourhood drinks in alleyways.
Opening post straight away.
Painting gazing. Pub lunch birthdays. Planning.
Quibbling quiz teams, gentle disagreement.
Reading in cafes, pubs, with people around.
Spontaneous changes. Swims. Seaside.
Talking to strangers about nothing + everything
Unspoken attractions, surprise paths crossed.
Venting to a friend and letting them vent back.
Water, being by it, in it, letting it calm me.
X-rated dreams.
Years of work, fun and time away plotted out.
Zoos, or the possibility of a long nose.

Sarah L. Dixon

The Way Ahead - Chris Sims

Back to Nature

A pool of sunlight on the forest floor.
I stand in it like one about to be
baptised. When I was young I wanted more
but age has taught me how to live with less,
to value what I have and start to see
the forest whole in all its loveliness

where in a clearing I surprise a deer
who looks up briefly and then walks away
though his the better claim to linger here.
I follow at a distance. He turns round
but shows no fear, just curious I'd say
to know what kind of creature shares this ground –

a kindred spirit or an enemy?
I choose a different path. The air is filled
with birdsong, manna falling from the trees,
and I emerge to blue sky, drifting cloud,
a pair of dappled horses in a field
who stand together with their grey heads bowed.

Philip Lyons

The Joy of Waking Up

to the chatter of birds and one, insistent song
tuneful, bursting

and I'm back at your bedside
to those months when you couldn't sit

unaided, your shrinking face, bold eyes
searching the room.

I touch your cheek. Your jaw softens, you
become a smile

we welcome another day.

Marg Roberts

A Different Future

If you're struggling under lockdown,
try not to feel so blue,
have faith that things will change
and together we'll get through.

We can create a *different* future,
a normal that is *new*,
where we value connections with people,
over profit and new shoes.

Replacing endless schedules,
with chatting over a brew,
changing clothes made from plastic
to those from hemp, or bamboo.

A world where we value nature,
stage an environmental coup,
A world with less pollution,
and a sky that is more blue.

How can we shift our focus,
change our world views?
Will all this become reality?
Well that is up to you.

Marcus Clark

Homo Hunter: A Dream

Hunting for shelter from the rain, I came
across a cave that would do for the Winter.

A wearying sun winked on a notch in the wall
like the eye of a deer, and again on what might
have been a mouth, and I had to draw it in as
a smile, and, before I knew what I had done,
a deer stood, entire.

By then, the sun was down and the reed lamp
flickered low, ready to retire, but the moon rose,
bright, as if it might be calling me out into the
cold night, to hunt the creature drawn on the wall,
now, out of my sight.

She stood at the mouth of the cave as if sent
as an answer to prayer, and I hewed her down.

Then, I saw her as part of a web of life:
she knew that I had to kill, to eat, as did
the sun and moon, and I thanked them all.
For I was the last to survive of a tribe killed
by strangers with flint knives.

Had I not taken this axe left in a brother's back,
I would not have survived, now, to feed and sleep …
Only, the tide was rising, the sea sweeping through
this dry sandy floor, where it had never been before
and I had to move on up to a higher cave.

Then men gathered around me and made me their slave.
Perhaps, like the deer, I should have surrendered my life?
Instead, I surrendered to the will of these men, traders of
flints from afar, weapons too severe for we creatures here
to survive their instinct to drive us extinct.

This is who I am: they sacrificed me to their gods, hoping to
be saved from extinction, when they saw men coming with
horses and chariots. How Homo Hunter has come on: how
reverently you lift and examine my bones, learn where and
when and how I lived and even know the extinct animals I
lived among!

You talk of 'Great' empires, but you know that greatness is, as
yet, to come, when Homo Hunter's drive towards extinction
is undone.

M. Anne Alexander

Pushing Back Night

Long hard days,
weary ways -
though not for all –
those who sacrifice.

Kiss your child.
Close the door,
ready to fight
this virulent war.

You're the air,
night after night
watching, with care—
brave until light.

Carry the load
above and beyond
lending kind hands
throughout the land.

Long hard days,
weary ways -
pushing back night,
doing what's right,

braving the fight,
longing for light,
willing to cope,
waiting for hope!

Thanks be to you—
thank you!
We live our lives
in joy and love.

Lizzie Ballagher

*Words written for music by composer Richard Hubbert in tribute
to the work of key workers and NHS staff.*

Weaving in Re-reading Eavan Boland in a Lockdown World 2
'A Woman without a County'

No, not for years, her books stack up on my shelves.
Longing for the fields of home I take down two today.
Open the random page.
'What do we grieve for
when we leave a count/r/y
and live for years in another one?'

I was a child
when we moved to the New Home.
Then moon years later
to the county town here.
I didn't know what now is clear.

'It is time to go back to where I came from'.
Yes, the blackbirds, a robin, sing full-tilt
and lilacs spill over the neighbouring fence,
but the low-fenced screened garden forms four-square walls,
and out there the beast is preying
raging inside other houses in nearby streets.

We all have our wobble days
mine, last week.
We know what's missed we're longing for
and we walk our allotted round
then wait through lockdown's longest nights.

Words are failing us,
there must be another side
that one where once we lived,
the one out over Blackdown's
western horizons
and all the still children there
the rainbows over the
thin blue somewhere
boundary line.

Julie Sampson

Masked - Chris Sims

Delphinium Blue

Delphinium Blue

It wasn't necessary to go to the garden centre
it was the fields that allured and the walk through
the early songs of summer. Social distancing was easily
managed: people polite and stepping into the ploughed
earth with a smile and a *Good Afternoon*.
The dog enjoyed himself; a walk's a walk after all.

But it was necessary to go to the garden centre
for I didn't have a delphinium, and I needed one
in that particular blue of cornflowers and the sea
off the coast of Corfu. I've never been to Corfu
but can imagine it, if I try not to think about the families
adrift in small boats off Lesbos.

And it wasn't actually a garden centre but a nursery
surrounded by farms and trees and you'd never know
it was there.
The thing is – if you visit a garden centre (or a nursery)
on a Sunday afternoon, you forget you've not got the car
and there we were ploughing through the fields
with plant pots and carrier bags and rucksacks
and the dog on his lead stopping not once but twice
for a poo   and the head of the delphinium bouncing
off my shoulder almost ready to bloom.

I can't remember wondering if the sky was blue
but if it wasn't there will be another
somewhere soon, even bluer.

Maggie Harris

250

Staying at Home

Woken at dawn by an unsleeping child
I pat the head, reset the night
lured by the light through the blinds
I pause
recall another morning
yawning into being
the drive to the airport
an early flight
excitement and nausea
the unscheduled rise
cold feet in sandals
a holiday hat, inconvenient now
inadequate seat belts fasten in laps
the body unprepared
lends itself to the sky.

Emily Reynolds

Isolation

It has been 53 days since I last saw my mother
but texts and calls crackle and spit
through pylons and speakers
as quick as unhealthy thoughts form and fire from
one neuron to the next in her mind,
like a derailed engine crashing through a station
at 3am, unwelcome but on schedule,
keeping her awake and afraid.

Between these frantic missives
frustration bleeds from my clenched hands to my fingertips;
moon-shaped scars on my palms
mark the passing of hours more accurately
than the crosses I forget to mark
on the kitchen calendar
(as if I have need of knowing what day of the week
just passed me by).

As she whispers her fears from 8 postcodes away,
of postmen outside doors that have not welcomed fresh air
for weeks let alone parcels and bills,
I fill my lungs with smoke and breathe
out assurances until
the cigarettes I clutch like the fingers of God
are burned down to the brand name.
And so am I.

Emily Fox

Nave

Crucifixions, endless godly scenes
genuflections, one knee dropped
to the floor in reverence.
In the church of Santa Maria Novella
where I have visited many times
the vast interior is breathtaking
not least of all Giotto's crucifix
suspended in mid air
the detail extraordinary.
Difficult to move away
your whole body tensing
at this moment of death.
I read that this stunning piece
took seven years to restore
using microscopes, how finicky
that labour of love, to stick with it
so we might stand wordless, in wonder.

Eileen Carney Hulme

Bumper Crop - Patricia McElroy

Writers' Retreat

Where the stillness of a summer's afternoon falls
lightly like the wisteria, lilac against pale stone;

where the sundial's silent measuring of shadowfall
whispers an irresistible summons;

where mayflies shimmer over a gold and green
dappled lake, appearing and disappearing sudden as a dream;

where poppies and cornflowers bob and sway
in the meadow by the war cemetery gates;

I found a walled garden, deserted except for the murmur
of bees, opened my notebook and began to write.

Anna Avebury

Lifting Restrictions

Now the darkness fades behind
me

The light that shone through the
mouth

Of a seeming endless
tunnel

Has
arrived

Not in a silver-wrapped parcel as
expected

But more
prosaically

in fleeting glimpses of a former
time

Clouded in a veil of
fog

Obscuring an uncertain
future

Here I stand
alone.

Thrown back out
broken.

Into a world that can never be
fixed

Aoife Doyle

Escape

The dog's tail has become my fingers,
I can't get purchase on the garden gate.

I need to leave,
but the dog wants to play,

I squeeze the tail, fingers become fur.
I'm thrust left, my head in the perennials,
to the right, I'm tangled in t-shirts
released from a boil wash.

C'mon dog, I cannot walk you today.
Neighbours appear, they bang spoons
against pans. The dog thinks they are
banging for him.

He starts to run.

Dog, dear dog, stop.
You do not understand.

The garden gate, the gate
that makes the dog happy

is behind us.

Stephen Lightbown

Waste

the bin woman is retiring
from tipping rubbish on unstable land
where crows look forward to building
nests for the future

she'll refuse to buy anything packaged
dig an organic allotment
peaches will grow against a stone wall
as the climate warms
she will see the fruit blush
tenderly stroke the velvety skin

Moira Garland

The Playground

Three yellow roses – perhaps four, not more –
among a range of shrubberies and trees
changing colour drew my eye towards –

or I should say back towards them since they
stood at the end of summer, at the end of a row
of terraces fronting the playground, empty now

that all the children were back at school
except for the unlucky few self-isolated at home
with a cough that was just a cough, the usual

cold and sniffles for this time of year only
this year wasn't usual. A spring rider,
a blue elephant with a yellow handle for an ear,

stood side-on to me, glaring with one eye.
The bench was wet with rain so I patted
the latticework with kitchen towel to dry it

and perched at one end to have a cigarette.
Yellow roses, my mother's favourite.
It was a beautiful morning, not cold at all.

It was a playground for solitude and pigeons,
for a quiet smoke and self-congratulation
on surviving, and nothing to do with isolation.

Mimi Khalvati

Do Not Proceed with Caution

Bang the drums and charge the pistons,
ignite the engines and switch on all systems.

Throw open the duvet and leave the bed unmade.
Put the kettle on and dance to the morning hit parade

Let the cat out,
take the dog off the lead,
slam the door behind you and do take heed:
that the rain has passed and today it will be bright spells.

Uncork the champagne;
tear open a packet of fireworks as you'll be seeing them again.

Do not proceed with caution.
Today will not be the day you fall ill with exhaustion.

Ignore the traffic lights as they're all suspended,
pending further notice till the celebrations have ended.

Coalesce with strangers round a street artist - pop a few quid in the jar,
when the crowd scatters fist-pump a bloke you saw from afar.

Disembark from a conga train when a girl you like all dressed in
blue breaks the chain and gets off too.

Take her hand, find a place to sit;
fall in love on that balmy evening wrapped in a warm Gulf Stream
blanket

Smoke a cigarette, a second and a third
offer the rest round to the jolly herd.

Watch those fireworks open like umbrellas and before too soon
dance like the owl and pussycat by the light of the moon.

Alex Smith

Inheritance

I have been wondering what I have to leave my son. I can't leave a house, a garden in springtime. I can barely leave him a wardrobe; just piles of clothes, something for every occasion. I know he loves the sequins and rainbows but forgive him, he's only four. I've gifted him my blue eyes, a curve of cheek and squiggly hair, passed down these generations of women. I can leave him this land; the dales of Yorkshire, the kiss of gorse on the moor. It's not mine but it is the bones that run through us. I can leave him a turn of phrase, the catch tone shifts in his voice just like mine. I can leave the memory of these shut-in days, with such love and fever and football in the deserted sunlit park.

Jem Henderson

Autumn - Susan Jane Sims

The Skyness

Flame of autumn was sown
On the hill far away
Warming the hearts with leaves of red, yellow, and glitter
It catches up with a bay steed, on the clouds of meadows
It will carry the news of the souls crying up into the circles of sky

Anna Maria Mickiewicz

Brief biographies for contributors

Shanta Acharya's latest collections are *Imagine: New and Selected Poems)* Harper Collins, 2017) and *What Survives is the Singing* (Indigo Dreams, 2020). www.shantaacharya.com

M. Anne Alexander is an active member of the Poetry Society's Enfield Stanza Group. Her poetry explores restorative relationships with our natural and spiritual worlds.

James Andrew is a Scottish poet who has had three books of poetry published as well as four novels. He is working on a fifth.

Moira Andrew 's latest collections are *Geese and Daughters* (IDP) *Looking Through Water* (Poetry Space) and *Imagine a Kiss* (D&W). She has also written educational books and books for children.

Anna Avebury lives in St Albans where she works in the central library. She is a member of local group, Ver Poets.

Dorothy Baird is a counsellor and creative writing tutor who lives in Edinburgh. Her latest poetry collection is *Mind the Gap* (Indigo Dreams Press Ltd).

Yvonne Baker has been published widely in magazines. Her work has been included in Second Light, Paper Swans and Emma Press anthologies.

Lizzie Ballagher's work has appeared in magazines & webzines on either side of the Atlantic. Find her blog at https:lizzieballagherpoetry.wordpress.com/

Verona Bass was encouraged by local Bath Artists and Writers group to write poetry. A Memoir Trilogy celebrates growing up on farms in South Africa.

Paul Beech, writing in North Wales, specialises in traditional Japanese poetry forms. He is a winner of the *Museum of Haiku Literature Award*.

Denise Bennett, poet and tutor, widely published - has three collections: *Planting the Snow Queen* and *Parachute Silk*, Oversteps Books, and *Water Chits* by Indigo Dreams.

Daniel Benson lives in Surrey with his young family. He enjoys combining visits to the royal parks to explore, climb trees and practice his photography.

Johanna Boal has published two collections of poetry, *Cardboard City*, (Poetry Space, 2014) and *Fizz and Hiss*, (Maytree Press, 2019) Publications online include Ink, Sweat and Tears, Edinburgh Festival Poetry Competition 2019.

Anne Boileau worked as translator, interpreter and language teacher. Her collection *Dreams of Flight* (Orphean Press, 2019) illustrated by Belinda King, includes translations from German.

Ama Bolton is a Poetry Society Stanza rep. She lives in Somerset with a sculptor and a hen.

Connie Ramsay Bott's poetry and fiction have been published in Britain and America. Her novel *Girl* Without Skin was published by Cinnamon Press in 2017.

Alison Brackenbury's selected poems: *Gallop* was published by Carcanet in 2019. Her website is at www.alisonbrackenbury.co.uk.

Carole Bromley's latest publications are a pamphlet, *Sodium 136* (Calder Valley) and a new collection, *The Peregrine Falcons of York Minster* (Valley Press).

Chaucer Cameron's forthcoming pamphlet *'In an Ideal World I'd Not Be Murdered'* will be published by Against the Grain 2021.

Alison Campbell was longlisted in Paper Swans pamphlet competition. Most recently her poems have appeared in Artemis, The Poetry Village and Pennine Platform (November).

Susan Castillo-Street is Harriet Beecher Stowe Professor Emerita, King's College London. A Southern expat, she has lived in the UK for many years. She has published four collections of poems.

Marcus Clark has been writing poetry from his hometown of Bristol since the year 2000 on a wide range of subjects from stars to teaspoons.

Rachael Clyne is a psychotherapist from Glastonbury. Her recent pamphlet, *Girl Golem* (4Word Press) is about her migrant background and sense of otherness.

Claire Grace Coleman lives and works for a charity in Somerset. She has been published in anthologies, poetry magazines and on-line by Literature Works.

Rose Cook lives in Devon. Her latest book is *Shedding Feathers* (Hen Run, Grey Hen Press, 2020).

Martyn Crucefix's most recent publications are *Cargo of Limbs* (Hercules Editions, 2019) *and These Numbered Days,* translations of the poems of Peter Huchel (Shearsman, 2019) - http://www.martyncrucefix.com.

During lockdown **Judy Dinnen** has been involved in a wild life project, a book of poems and prayers and a lockdown poem for a dance school in Australia.

Sarah L Dixon, lives in a Huddersfield valley with her ten year old son. She loves being in and by water. **www.thequietcompere.co.uk**.

Brian Docherty is the Beach Bard of St. Leonards. His books include *A Year On The Marina (2017)*, and *Blue To The Edge (2020).*

Michael Docker lives and works in Bristol. He has been writing (mostly poetry) for about forty years.

Aoife Doyle is a hospital doctor in Dublin, eye specialist and newcomer to the world of writing. A lover of all to do with colour, light and the natural world.

Margaret Eddershaw is a UK poet, whose publications include two collections, one pamphlet and a full length performance poem about George Eliot.

Pat Edwards is a writer, reviewer, workshop leader . She hosts Verbatim open mic and curates Welshpool Poetry Festival. Two pamphlets: *Only Blood* (Yaffle); *Kissing in the Dark* (IDP).

Carol Fenwick is a writer from Kent. You can find her poetry in The Sunday Tribune and The International Times among other publications.

Beverley Ferguson, Textile and Mixed Media Artist at Bath Artists' Studios. Poetry Space Ltd. publications: *Breaking Through,* 2013 and *Flowers in the Blood*, 2014.

Michael Forester is author of ten books and five poetry collections and is a regular contributor to international poetry anthologies. His work can be viewed at www.michaelforester.co.uk/books.

Emily Fox is a newcomer, currently completing her Creative Writing degree. Her poem *Seven Pomegranate Seeds* was shortlisted for the 2020 Bridport Prize.

Marilyn Francis lives and writes poetry in Radstock, once part of the Somerset coalfield. Some of her poems have been published, but more remain in her head.

Wendy French's latest collection, *Bread Without Butter*, *bara heb fenyn* was published by Rockingham Press, 2020. She facilitates writing sessions at UCH Macmillan Cancer Centre.

A *Leeds Peace Poetry 2016* competition winner, **Moira Garland's** work appears in *The North,* in anthologies including *How the Stones Fell Open, Bloody Amazing,* and www.poetryandcovid.com, @moiragauthor.

Victoria Gatehouse is a poet and medical researcher. Her latest pamphlet *The Mechanics of Love* was a Laureate's Choice for 2019.

Leela Gautam, a retired doctor, writes poetry for pleasure. Her poems have been published in magazines and newspapers in India. she has also contributed to Poetry Space online Showcase Quarterly.

Rosina Georgiou is an English teacher and PhD student in North London. She is currently writing her first novel and researching constructions of femininity in contemporary British chick-lit narratives.

Caroline Gill lives in Suffolk. Her first full-length poetry collection will be published in 2021 with The Seventh Quarry Press (Swansea). www.carolinegillpoetry.com.

Sarah Gillespie is an artist printmaker based in Devon. Her recent work on moths has been featured in both *The Guardian* and *BBC Online.*

A translator living in France, **Mary Gilonne** has won or been placed in many competitions. Published widely, her pamphlet 'Incidentals' (4Word Press) appeared in 2018.

Eileen Anne Gordon: *Without a Light* is Eileen's first poem to appear in an anthology. She recently had two poems shortlisted in the Fingal Festival (Ireland) Poetry Prize Competition.

Sheila Gosling is a grandmother who now has the time to play with words, create poems for pleasure and, stand and stare.

Greenwood: David a musician and Susan an artist came to visit the UK from France and were locked down in Dorset. Now they are planning to stay.

Wendy Halsted is a music therapist, Interfaith minister and artist in Sussex. During Lockdown, she lived with her mum in the Wirral.

Ruth Hanchett's pamphlet *Some Effects Of Brilliance* was published in 2019. She writes in various poetic forms and won the Segora Poetry Competition 2016.

Stuart Handysides runs the Ware Poets competition. His poems have appeared in several magazines.

Deborah Harvey's fifth poetry collection, *Learning Finity,* will be published by Indigo Dreams in 2021. Deborah is co-director of *The Leaping Word* poetry consultancy.

Maggie Harris' latest poetry collection is *On Watching a Lemon Sail the Sea.* (Cane Arrow Press) www.maggieharris.co.uk.

Jacqueline Haskell's novel *The Auspice* was a finalist in the 2018 Bath Novel Award, and her poetry collection *Stroking Cerberus* was published by Myriad Editions, 2020.

Pippa Hawkins attends a number of poetry groups in Bristol. Cinnamon Press published her first pamphlet *The Care Line* in 2018.

Caroline Heaton's poetry has appeared in journals, anthologies and a collaborative pamphlet, *The Bone-House,* and set to music by composer Malcolm Hill.

Jem Henderson has an MA in Creative Writing from York St. John University. She has been published in Civic Leicester's Black Lives Matter anthology and various publications online.

Angi Holden's writing for adults and children includes the *Victoria Baths Splash Fiction Prize* winner, and *Spools of Thread,* the *MMB Poetry Pamphlet Prize* winner.

Jane Hughes loves her garden, her family and she is especially passionate about music! All of these inspire her writing.

Eileen Carney Hulme lives in the north east of Scotland and is a multi prize-winning poet with three collections published.

Michael Hutchinson is well-known in the Reading poetry scene and in 2016 contributed the title poem to the University of Reading Creative Arts Anthology.

Rosie Jackson lives in Devon. Her 2020 books of poems are *Two Girls and a Beehive,* about Stanley Spencer, and *Aloneness Is a Many-Headed Bird,* with Dawn Gorman.

David C. Johnson is a Bristol poet, BBC radio playwright and poetry slam champion. His most recent poetry collection is *Earwig in the Radio* (Paralalia 2015) (www.davidcjohnsonpoet.com).

Rema Jyothirmayi is a consultant oncologist at the Kent Oncology Centre. She has recently started writing poetry and *Empathy* is her first published poem.

Zannah Kearns' poems can be found in *Finished Creatures, South, Poetry Birmingham Literary Journal and Under the Radar,* and online at Atrium and Ink, Sweat & Tears. @zannahkearns.

Mimi Khalvati has nine collections with Carcanet Press, including *The Meanest Flower*, shortlisted for the T.S. Eliot prize. Her most recent *Afterwardness*, is a PBS Winter Wild Card. She is a Fellow of the RSL.

Julie King is a mum, a nana, a hippy, a lover, a wanderer in nature and wisdom, an eclectic old soul, a cat lover, a dabbler in all things, a master of nothing and nobody.

Stephen Kingsnorth, retired to Wales from ministry in the Methodist Church, has had 200 pieces published by on-line poetry sites, printed journals and anthologies. https://poetrykingsnorth.wordpress.com/.

Pru Kitching has two pamphlets and several magazine publications in her name. Now working on her first collection, *Never Wear Any Colour But Blue,* she lives in Newcastle.

Morag Kiziewicz is a columnist for *Tears in the Fence*, a Wells Fountain Stanza member and co-editor of Cascade, University of Bath.

Andrew Lawrence been walking round Bath for 50 years now and writing poetry for nearly all of that time. Retirement gives even more opportunities!

Stephen Lightbown is a Blackburn born, Bristol based poet. He writes extensively but not exclusively about his life as a wheelchair user.

Toby Litt is Reader in Creative Writing at Birkbeck College. His most recent novel was *Patience* (Galley Beggar Press).

Alison Lock's poetry seeks to connect an inner world through a love of the natural world to unearth the relationship between humans and their environment.

Hannah Lowe's first poetry collection *Chick* (Bloodaxe, 2013) won the Michael Murphy Memorial Award. In 2014, she was named as one of 20 Next Generation British poets. Her third collection, *The Kids, is* due with Bloodaxe in 2021. twitter: hannahlowepoet. web: hannahlowe.me.

Philip Lyons lives in Bristol. He is the author of one full-length collection, *Like It Is* (Poetry Space, 2011).

Mark Maddrell - gardener, poet, healer and musician .

Alwyn Marriage's eleven books include poetry, fiction and non-fiction. Formerly university lecturer and Director of two international NGOs, she is Managing Editor of Oversteps and research fellow at Surrey University. www.marriages.me.uk/alwyn

Patricia McElroy lives in Brussels and has been painting for many years. She works mainly in acrylic and is inspired by life in all its forms.

Alanna McIntyre runs a creative writing class in her local community centre and during lockdown found art very therapeutic.

Jane McLaughlin's short stories and poetry are widely published and have won several awards; her poetry collection *Lockdown* is published by Cinnamon Press. https://facebook.com/janemclaughlinpage/'.

Lucie Meadows writes for her pleasure and wellbeing. She facilitates meditation & writing workshops and is currently an MSc student of Creative Writing for Therapeutic Purposes.

Anna Maria Mickiewicz (http://faleliterackie.com) is a Polish-born poet, writer and editor She edits the magazine *The Literary Memoir, and Contemporary Writers of Poland (USA).*

Sandeep Kumar Mishra is a writer, poet and lecturer in English Literature. He has edited a collection of poems by various poets - Pearls (2002) and written a professional guidebook -How to be (2016) and a collection of poems and art—*Feel My Heart* (2016).

 Sarah Mnatzaganian is an Anglo-Armenian poet. Highly commended in the 2019 Mslexia/PBS pamphlet competition and shortlisted for the Poetry Business pamphlet competition 2016/17.

Steven Mwalusi is a Zambian business researcher/poet. He is father to ne daughter Eliana and has been writing poetry as a pastime since his teens.

Ruth O'Callaghan: 11 collections, Hawthornden Fellow, mentor, workshop leader, interviewer, competition adjudicator, runs 2 London poetry venues, translated into 6 languages, reads USA, Asia, Europe.

Based in Sherborne since 2017, **Mark Pender** paints a variety of subjects but specialises in fantasy or fairy tale oil or acrylic paintings, usually dark or humorous, sometimes both.

Miranda Pender lives in Sherborne, and works intuitively to create quirky, colourful collage paintings - her favourite subjects are ammonites and labyrinths. She is also a singer and songwriter.

Geralyn Pinto is a fiction writer and poet from Mangalore, south India. She has been published and won prizes nationally and internationally.

Ann Preston is a member of Bath Artists and Writers Group. Her poems have been shortlisted in the *Wells* and the *Charles Causley Poetry Competitions.*

Kate Pursglove has always loved poetry (including Tennyson's!) and since retirement has had more time for reading, writing and reviewing, and for facilitating a poetry group in Reading – a life-saver during lockdown.

Mohammed Qasim is a part time writer from Birmingham, UK. He hopes his words will help inspire a better tomorrow, one based on equality and social cohesion.

Lesley Quayle is a poet, editor and folk/blues singer. Her most recent pamphlet, published by 4Word, is Black Bicycle. https://www.4word.org/ .

Peter Reason seeks to link the tradition of nature writing with the ecological crisis of our times, drawing on scientific, ecological, philosophical and spiritual sources.

Emily Reynolds lives in Bristol with her family. She spends her days working with new mothers and writes after bedtime when everything is quiet.

Jenny Robb from Liverpool, has been writing poetry since retiring. This year she has been published in both online and print magazines and in poetry anthologies.

Marg Roberts survives and thrives during the pandemic by writing poetry and prose. Walking and cycling help her adjust to not meeting family and friends.

Adele V. Robinson is a Lancaster University English graduate and a founding member of Lancashire Dead Good Poets. She gained Arts Council funding for the *Walking on Wyre* project in 2014.

Julie Sampson's collections are *Tessitura* (Shearsman, 2013) and *It Was When It Was When It Was* (Dempsey & Windle, 2018).

Peter Scalpello is a queer poet and sexual health therapist from Glasgow. His debut pamphlets will be published by Broken Sleep Books in March 2021. Tweets @p_scalpello.

Myra Schneider is consultant to the Second Light Network and tutors for The Poetry School. Her latest collection is *Lifting the Sky* (Ward Wood 2018)

Andy Scotson lives in Daventry with his wife Jeanette. He writes a lot of poetry and has had one pamphlet published.

Chris Sims is based in Dorset where he runs Tangerine Cafe jointly with Sue. He has a passion for walking, cycling and photography.

Susan Jane Sims, a Hawthornden fellow, runs Poetry Space from her Dorset home, alongside Tangerine Cafe & Gallery with her husband Chris. Her most recent collection is *Splitting Sunlight* (Dempsey & Windle, 2019).

Alex Smith works in the City and in his spare time enjoys reading and writing poetry to elevate the soul and reflect on the most important things in life: relationships with people and the planet.

Anne Stewart runs the poet showcase www.poetrypf.co.uk and is administrator for Second Light. Her latest of four poetry collections is *The Last Parent* (SLP, 2019).

Tessa Strickland founded independent publisher Barefoot Books in 1993. She now runs a private psychotherapy practice in NE Somerset and mentors emergent writers.

Janet Sutherland lives in Lewes, Sussex, and has four collections from Shearsman Books, the most recent of which is *Home Farm* (2019).

Robin Thomas lives in Reading. His most recent collection is *Momentary*

Turmoil (Cinnamon, 2018). A further collection will be published by Cinnamon in early 2021.

Denni Turp lives in north Wales. Her work has been published in poetry magazines, anthologies, and webzines.

Susannah Violette a Pushcart Prize nominee, has had poems placed or commended in various prizes and appears in many publications worldwide. She lives in Germany.

Jo Waterworth lives in Glastonbury, Somerset, where she reads a lot, writes a little and cares for grandchildren when not prevented by lockdowns.

Irene Watson is a mid-career fine artist, poet and lecturer. She lives in rural Perthshire and works on her writing and artwork full time.

Maureen Weldon, Lives in Wales. Published six poetry pamphlets, latest *Midnight Robin,* Poetry Space Press. Next pamphlet due in New Year 2021, Red Squirrel Press.

Richard Westcott, a retired GP, lives in Devon where he worked. His pamphlet is available from Indigo Dreams and he blogs at richardwestcottspoetry.

Carol Whitfield has been writing for over twenty years. Poems have been placed in competitions and magazines, sometimes under her maiden name of Beadle.

Catherine Whittaker has many poems published in anthologies and magazines, has a degree in Creative Writing and tutors Poetry and Creative Writing (on Zoom!).

Dilys Wood founded Second Light Network for women poets in 1994. She has co-edited 5 anthologies of women's poetry and ARTEMIS poetry journal.

UK-born **Natalie Wood** emigrated to Galilee, Israel in 2010 from where she blogs and composes flash and micro-fiction and free verse.

John Wright Poet since 1960s. M. Creative Writing, Uni. of Kent (2014) Member Eastbourne Poetry Cafe group and The Downland Poets Pub *Ikenography* 2015 *Scribble, scribble* 2020.

Pam Zinnemann-Hope has published two collections, '*On Cigarette Papers*' & '*Foothold*', both with Ward Wood. She lives in West Dorset.

Index of poets, writers and artists